PUBLIC PROFILES

# Influential
# Hip-Hop Artists

KENDRICK LAMAR, NICKI MINAJ AND OTHERS

THE NEW YORK TIMES EDITORIAL STAFF

Published in 2019 by The New York Times® Educational Publishing in association with The Rosen Publishing Group, Inc.
29 East 21st Street, New York, NY 10010

First Edition

**The New York Times**
Alex Ward: Editorial Director, Book Development
Phyllis Collazo: Photo Rights/Permissions Editor
Heidi Giovine: Administrative Manager

**Rosen Publishing**
Megan Kellerman: Managing Editor
Julia Bosson: Editor
Greg Tucker: Creative Director
Brian Garvey: Art Director

**Cataloging-in-Publication Data**
Names: New York Times Company.
Title: Influential hip-hop artists: Kendrick Lamar, Nicki Minaj and others / edited by the New York Times editorial staff.
Description: New York : New York Times Educational Publishing, 2019. | Series: Public profiles | Includes glossary and index.
Identifiers: ISBN 9781642821666 (library bound) | ISBN 9781642821659 (pbk.) | ISBN 9781642821673 (ebook)
Subjects: LCSH: Rap musicians—United States—Juvenile literature. | Hip-hop—Juvenile literature. | Rap (Music)—Juvenile literature.
Classification: LCC ML3531.I565 2019 | DDC 782—dc23

*Manufactured in the United States of America*

**On the cover:** The Tools of War Park Jam at St. Nicholas Park was themed "digger's delight," in which D.J.s, most of them using 45's, spun older and more obscure music; Todd Heisler/ The New York Times.

# Contents

**CHAPTER 3**

# Kendrick Lamar

CHAPTER 4

# Drake

CHAPTER 5

# Cardi B

# Kanye West

# Introduction

WHEN THE WINNERS of the 2018 Pulitzer Prize were announced, one category in particular caused a stir: Kendrick Lamar had become the first hip-hop artist to receive the Pulitzer Prize for Music, which he won for his album "DAMN."

Jurors later told reporters that the decision had been unanimous. For observers and critics, the decision seemed to mark a major change in the perception of hip-hop. "DAMN." had already received widespread critical acclaim for its musical sophistication as well as Lamar's innovative lyricism. Lamar's reputation had been elevated by his earlier album "To Pimp a Butterfly," whose political messaging made it a symbol of black activism and which earned him a number of Grammy nominations and wins. But the Pulitzer Prize demonstrated something different: hip-hop was finally receiving the recognition it deserved.

Hip-hop has its origins in the 1970s in the Bronx, where early progenitors included Afrika Bambaataa, Grandmaster Flash and DJ Kool Herc. It has since grown in popularity, evolving over the years into a diverse and dynamic musical genre that includes aspects of beatboxing, rapping and sampling of tracks. Even more, hip-hop has become an identifiable culture, with associated styles, language and heroes.

Like other forms of black music, hip-hop has operated as both a form of resistance and an artistic refuge for the black community. While the audience of hip-hop music is diverse, the vast majority of its stars are people of color. As such, many of the genre's themes are connected to black life and culture. While hip-hop lyrics often detail an artist's status, biography and material wealth, they also reflect a political awareness, resulting in a legacy of pointed activism and vital protest.

Kendrick Lamar in Los Angeles in March 2015.

The articles in this book highlight the careers and works of six of hip-hop's major stars: Jay-Z, Kendrick Lamar, Nicki Minaj, Drake, Cardi B and Kanye West. These artists embody different aspects of a diverse and ever-evolving industry: Jay-Z, who has been releasing records since the mid-90s, has shaped the sound of hip-hop through his work with his Roc Nation label, while Cardi B is one of the newest voices on the scene.

The popularity of these stars has resulted in conflict as well as acclaim. Kanye West has long been one of hip-hop's most prominent and controversial voices, landing in trouble for his off-the-cuff and unpredictable statements. Nicki Minaj famously feuded with the pop star Taylor Swift. As the articles in this book demonstrate, all of these musicians have had to negotiate the very real consequences that accompany extreme fame and wealth.

As these artists have reached superstardom, their influence has affected areas of culture well beyond just the music industry. Kanye

West has shaken up the fashion world with his Yeezy fashion line, and Jay-Z has become a well-known investor and entrepreneur. From business ventures to Pulitzer Prizes, these artists have had an indisputable impact on American society.

Even as hip-hop has received widespread cultural attention, it is also in a state of transition. Long dominated primarily by male artists, more and more female rappers are rising to prominence, contributing to new musical styles and lyrical subjects. And as the expansion of free platforms such as Soundcloud and YouTube allows undiscovered artists to build an audience, the genre continues to expand and evolve. One thing is for certain: hip-hop is an art form on the rise.

# CHAPTER 1

# Jay-Z

Jay-Z (born Shawn Carter) released his first album "Reasonable Doubt" in 1996, topping the Billboard charts and going platinum. Since then, Jay-Z has authored more than a dozen records and produced many others, cementing his status as a hip-hop icon. His influence extends beyond his music: he has founded a record label, bought a stake in the Brooklyn Nets and made a name for himself in artistic and philanthropic circles. The articles in this chapter highlight his career trajectory and reputation.

## 10 Years Wiser, Jay-Z Offers His Reflections of a Hustler

BY KELEFA SANNEH | JUNE 27, 2006

IF YOU REMEMBER the 90's right now, put one hand in the air right now.

That's a cleaned-up version of what Funkmaster Flex said as he warmed up the crowd in Radio City Music Hall on Sunday night. He asked, "How many people 25 and older?" And thousands of old-timers made some noise. This was a night devoted to ancient history, which explains why Jay-Z rolled onstage in a vintage automobile: a decade-old Lexus.

The occasion was the 10th anniversary of Jay-Z's debut album, "Reasonable Doubt," which is now widely — and properly — celebrated as a hip-hop classic. If his life had imitated one of his own dopeman narratives, his quick rise would have been followed by success, excess and a slow decline. (Or maybe, if he made one enemy too many, a quick one.) Instead, he got on top and stayed there; he was the rapper to

Jay-Z performs at a concert to celebrate the 10th anniversary of his first album, "Reasonable Doubt" at Radio City Music Hall on June 25, 2006, in New York City. He performed the album in its entirety with special guests.

beat even when he wasn't topping the charts. He retired in 2003 and became president of Def Jam Recordings, but no one believes he's gone for good. Back then he bragged about having "matching VCR's, a huge Magnavox." A decade later that boast sounds impressive in a way he couldn't have predicted: the flashy Brooklyn rapper has outgrown Magnavox and outlasted VCR's.

For this celebration, Jay-Z was joined by ?uestlove, the drummer from the Roots, and a band called the Illadelphonics. There was also an orchestra ("the Hustlers Symphony Orchestra," he said) and a D.J., Just Blaze. Together they evoked the three basic musical elements of "Reasonable Doubt": hard beats (the band), plush arrangements (the strings) and well-chosen samples (the D.J.).

Jay-Z and the musicians had what was billed as a rehearsal on Saturday night, at the Nokia Theater, though it turned into a concert: the tickets, priced at $100, disappeared immediately, and fans got their money's worth. And Sunday's show — the whole album, with the songs played in reverse order, plus half an hour of "bonus time," or greatest hits — was an extraordinary achievement. This might be the best hip-hop concert since — well, since Jay-Z's legendary 2003 show.

The decision to run the album backward was a smart one. The night started with the album's elegiac finale, "Regrets." And he built toward "Can't Knock the Hustle," an exuberant statement of purpose originally featuring Mary J. Blige; on Sunday Beyoncé filled in.

Sauce Money and Memphis Bleek, two other rappers with verses on the album, also appeared, although Jaz-O (then Big Jaz), Jay-Z's former mentor, was conspicuously absent. (In the new issue of XXL magazine, which includes an invaluable feature on the making of "Reasonable Doubt," Jaz-O says he's "very disappointed" that Jay-Z has "downplayed" his contribution to the album.) Foxy Brown, the rapper who has been battling hearing loss, appeared for "Ain't No"; she lost the beat, but persevered.

And what of Cristal? The Champagne company offended Jay-Z when its managing director gave an interview in which he seemed ungrateful about rappers' patronage. There were rumors that Jay-Z was going to remove all Cristal references from his rhymes. In "Dead Presidents II," he changed one line to, "Maybe this rosé will change your life." But he slipped up in "Can't Knock the Hustle": he was back to drinking "Cristal by the bottle." (Honest, he can stop any time he wants.)

Like most great hip-hop albums, "Reasonable Doubt" is designed to delight word nerds. Part of the genius of the album was that Jay-Z realized you could deliver complicated rhythms and rhymes in a casual, conversational voice. His predecessor, the Notorious B.I.G. (who was killed in 1997), loved to stretch out words to emphasize meter; Jay-Z did a little of that on Sunday, when he rapped both his and B.I.G.'s verses from their duet, "Brooklyn's Finest." (In XXL the hip-hop mogul Irv Gotti says that when Jay-Z and B.I.G. recorded that track, they were "very competitive"; each was gunning for the other.)

Jay-Z's tough but laid-back style, which would dominate New York hip-hop for the next decade, let rappers break down the competition without breaking a sweat. (Speaking of which, how did he stay so cool and composed on that hot stage, in that three-piece suit?) In "Dead Presidents II" he exhaled those tongue-twisting opening lines as if he were merely thinking out loud: "Who wanna bet us that we don't touch leathers/Stack cheddars forever/Live treacherous, all the et ceteras?"

Jay-Z took this conversational style to its logical extreme on "Friend or Foe," a prose monologue that scans:

*You're twitching. Don't do that, you're making me nervous.*
*My crew? Well, they do pack — them dudes is murderers.*
*So wouldja please put your hands back in sight?*
*They don't like to see me nervous. You can understand that, right?*

And in the geekiest moment of the night he added a new verse to "22 Two's," his literal-minded rhyme exercise. In the original he rhymed, "I been around this block too many times/Rocked too many rhymes/Cocked too many .9's too," and so on, until he hit 22. In the new verse he rhymed, "Roc-a-Fella forever, Hov for life/Classic debut, first album's four mics," and the video screen kept count until, inevitably, he hit 44 fours.

After a night like this it might be tempting to talk about how "Reasonable Doubt" was a singular achievement, about how 1996 was a special year for hip-hop, about how they don't make them like that any more. But "Reasonable Doubt" isn't really an anomaly: it's much better than most hip-hop albums of those days, or these, but it's not much different. It's the sound of a slick-talking hustler making old stories sound new and making a few bucks along the way. In 2006 an album like this is less likely to come from Brooklyn and more likely to come from, say, Atlanta. It might have fewer words and weirder beats. But the tradition is much the same. That's the most exciting thing about the "Reasonable Doubt" era: It's not over yet.

# The Anxiety of Being Influential

BY JON CARAMANICA | SEPT. 16, 2009

THE ONLY OBSESSION more intense than the one other rappers have with Jay-Z is the one Jay-Z has with them.

That he's an object of admiration, envy and scorn is obvious. His influence has become part of hip-hop's DNA, his legacy something every new rapper must synthesize and address.

At least that's what he reckons. The Jay-Z of "The Blueprint 3" (Roc Nation), which was released last Tuesday and sold 476,000 copies in its first week, sleeps with one eye open. "They can't focus on them, they be talkin' about me," he moans on the first song, "What We Talkin' About." "Talkin' about what I wear, talkin' about where I be."

In his real life Jay-Z comfortably does grown-up things: organizing and performing at a 9/11 charity concert at Madison Square Garden last Friday; playfully parrying marriage questions from David Letterman; delivering well-honed therapy-speak in an interview with Oprah Winfrey for her magazine; attending a Grizzly Bear show.

But Jay-Z spends so much of "The Blueprint 3," his 11th solo album, looking over his shoulder that it becomes blurry who's being stalked and who's the stalker. This is Jay-Z as paranoiac, grappling with the anxiety of being influential. And a nervous Jay-Z, it turns out, can be an effective one.

Jay-Z will turn 40 in a couple of months, and yet this album isn't much troubled by his advancing age, unlike his last few, which were lackadaisical victory laps. Instead the text of this album is durability and influence. (He is now the solo artist with the most No. 1 albums, 11, in Billboard history, surpassing Elvis Presley; he now trails only the Beatles over all.) "The thing that I can do is stretch the subject matter," he told XXL magazine this month, later adding, "We have to expand the genre."

And for the last few years that's what he's been attempting, bending and twisting it in all sorts of uncomfortable directions. The results have been his weakest albums, and also his least thoughtful. Maturity has not equated with grace.

On "The Blueprint 3" he has changed his approach. Instead of rapping for fans his own age he's back to targeting young people, except now he's talking down to them. Multiple songs here — "D.O.A. (Death of Auto-Tune)," "Off That," "On to the Next One," "Reminder" — essentially boil down to laundry lists of things Jay-Z doesn't like, to say nothing of things Jay-Z did before you did. Still, there's nothing as acidic as his boast on "Hovi Baby," from 2002: "If you did it, I done it before/You get it, I had it/Got mad at it and don't want it no more."

Here's what Jay-Z has forgotten, though: All that influence has paid dividends.

"Allow me to reintroduce myself," Young Jeezy raps at the beginning of "Real as It Gets," quoting Jay-Z's 2003 song "Public Service Announcement." But then the student takes the ball and runs with it: "At the same time reintroduce my wealth/At the same time rejuvenate the game." Young Jeezy taking a stab at improving on a Jay-Z lyric would have been unthinkable just a couple of years ago, but it was Jay-Z, his advocate, mentor and collaborator, who has helped Young Jeezy attempt something greater than being corner-obsessed and monotone.

"Blueprints for sale," Jay-Z says later in the song. "Follow in my footprints, you can't fail."

The same goes for Kanye West, a main recipient of Jay-Z's beneficence, who is an executive producer and producer of several songs on this album. With his clever and tart guest verses, Mr. West also enlivens the pair of songs he raps on, "Hate" and "Run This Town."

When one of his protégés is there to push him, Jay-Z is at his crispest, but alone he's less focused. Worse, this album marks the first time he's blatantly following in others' footsteps: teaming with Kid Cudi (following Mr. West, who initially recruited Kid Cudi last year to work on songs for, you guessed it, Jay-Z, which were deemed too outré), collaborating with Drake (after Lil Wayne), name-dropping Martin Margiela (Drake), using the sensual-rap revivalists the Inkredibles (Rick Ross).

So it's a mixed bag, which means this album has far less to do with "The Blueprint," which was released in 2001 and remains one of Jay-Z's most tonally consistent albums (if not his most thrilling), than with "Vol. 3 ...Life and Times of S. Carter," which preceded it by two years.

This is good news. "Vol. 3" was Jay-Z at his apex, brash and experimental and not yet complacent. In places on the new album he recaptures that energy. Swizz Beatz and Timbaland, longtime collaborators, return with sensational, off-kilter beats. On songs like "Young Forever" and "Already Home," Jay-Z tries out unusual flow patterns. And he revisits his dark side, giving the address of his old stash house on "Empire State of Mind" and, on "Thank You" — which recalls "Friend or Foe," the chiding, chilling narrative from his 1996 debut album, "Reasonable Doubt" — rapping:

> *Danger approaches, we're like wait, who's this?*
> *Let us save you some trouble, son: what size suit you is?*
> *This way after the Ruger shoots through a few clips*
> *You can lay in your casket just as you is*
> *We appreciate the target practices.*
> *We'll be sure to send flower baskets, kid.*

But Jay-Z proves unreliable with an emotionally tone-deaf third verse. "I was going to 9/11 them, but they didn't need the help," he raps of some rivals.

> *Not only did they brick, they put a building up as well*
> *Then ran a plane into that building and when that building fell*
> *Ran to the crash site with no mask and inhaled*
> *Toxins deep inside they lungs until both of them was filled.*

Yes, this is the rapper who, on the eighth anniversary of the Sept. 11 terrorist attacks, performed a concert for which all the ticket proceeds went to the New York Police and Fire Widows' and Children's Benefit Fund. It was an undeniable good deed, but also, more important, an opportunity for Jay-Z to move beyond himself.

That theme recurred throughout the night, during which Jay-Z often ceded the stage willingly: to his wife, Beyoncé; to Mr. West; to John Mayer, who was devastating, adding guitar to "U Don't Know" and "D.O.A. (Death of Auto-Tune)" as Jay-Z stared at him, agape.

The Madison Square Garden concert was one of three times in the past week he has allowed himself to be upstaged during a show. At the MTV Video Music Awards Lil Mama crashed his performance of "Empire State of Mind," and he barely seemed miffed. And on "The Jay Leno Show" his performance of "Run This Town" was swallowed whole by Mr. West, who outrapped him and outemoted him all at once.

Maybe, after all that intense focus on those focusing on him, Jay-Z's head is moving elsewhere.

Recently he discussed his next album, on which he's already working, with MTV: "I want to make the most experimental album that I've ever made." Does that mean covers of Deep Puddle Dynamics? No Age collaborations? Songwriting by Jandek and Pink Eyes? He needn't bother. Albums like "The Blueprint 3," an unexpected blend of maturity and youth, are risk enough.

# Jay-Z Deconstructs Himself

BY MICHIKO KAKUTANI  |  NOV. 22, 2010

IN THE SUMMER of 1978, when he was 9 years old and growing up in the Marcy housing projects in Brooklyn, Shawn Carter — aka Jay-Z — saw a circle of people gathered around a kid named Slate, who was "rhyming, throwing out couplet after couplet like he was in a trance, for a crazy long time — 30 minutes straight off the top of his head, never losing the beat, riding the handclaps" of the folks around him, trans-formed "like the church ladies touched by the spirit." Young Shawn felt gravity working on him, "like a planet pulled into orbit by a star": he went home that night and started writing his own rhymes in a note-book and studying the dictionary.

"Everywhere I went I'd write," Jay-Z recalls in his compelling new book, "Decoded." "If I was crossing a street with my friends and a rhyme came to me, I'd break out my binder, spread it on a mailbox or lamppost and write the rhyme before I crossed the street." If he didn't have his notebook with him, he'd run to "the corner store, buy some-thing, then find a pen to write it on the back of the brown paper bag." That became impractical when he was a teenager, working streets up and down the eastern corridor, selling crack, and he says he began to work on memorizing, creating "little corners in my head where I stored rhymes."

In time, that love of words would give Jay-Z more No. 1 albums than Elvis and fuel the realization of his boyhood dream: becoming, as he wrote in one of his earliest lyrics, the poet with "rhymes so provoca-tive" that he was the "key in the lock" — "the king of hip-hop."

Part autobiography, part lavishly illustrated commentary on the author's own work, "Decoded" gives the reader a harrowing portrait of the rough worlds Jay-Z navigated in his youth, while at the same time deconstructing his lyrics, in much the way that Stephen Sond-heim does in his new book, "Finishing the Hat."

"Decoded" is less a conventional memoir or artistic manifesto than an elliptical, puzzlelike collage: amid the photo-sharp reminiscences, there are impassioned music history lessons that place rap in a social and political context; enthusiastic shout-outs to the Notorious B.I.G. and Lauryn Hill; remedial lessons in street slang ("cheese" and "cheddar," the casual hip-hop tourist will learn, translate into "money"); and personal asides about the exhaustingly competitive nature of rap and the similarities between rap and boxing, and boxing and hustling drugs.

At the same time, "Decoded" is a book that highlights the richly layered, metaphoric nature of the author's own rhymes (even those about guns and girls and bling often turn out to have hidden meanings, stashed like "Easter eggs" in the weeds) — a book that underscores how the pressures of Jay-Z's former life as a dealer honed his gifts as a writer, including a survivor's appraising sense of character, an observer's eye for detail and a hustler's penchant for wordplay and control.

Jay-Z has mythologized his life before, of course — many of his most resonant lyrics, particularly those on his autobiographical masterpiece, "The Black Album," are works of willful self-dramatization. And the basic outlines of his Horatio Alger story are well known: his childhood in Bed-Stuy during the crack epidemic; his father's departure from the family, leaving him "a kid torn apart"; his career as a dealer, "tryin' to come up/in the game and add a couple of dollar signs to my name"; his debut album, "Reasonable Doubt," in 1996 (by which time, he has said, he "was the oldest 26-year-old you ever wanted to meet"); his ascent as a rap star, followed by his success as a producer, an entrepreneur and a chief executive ("I'm not a businessman/I'm a business, man.")

Confidence is hardly in short supply for Jay-Z. This is the writer, after all, whose nickname is Hova (as in Jay-Hova), the rapper who has boasted of being "Michael Magic and Bird all rolled in one," the "Sinatra of my day." But Jay-Z writes here that he's also tried, in his lyrics, to address emotions that "young men don't normally talk about with each other: regret, longing, fear and even self-reproach," and there are passages in this volume where the reader catches glimpses of the complicated, earnest artist behind the swaggering persona.

As in the lyrics, such passages are often half-hidden. His father's abandonment and the harsh code of the streets made Jay-Z, in his words, "a guarded person" — wary of feeling or exposing too much, and practiced in the art of detachment. And affecting moments of vulnerability (seeing his father many years later, he writes, was "like looking in a mirror," and it "made me wonder how someone could abandon a child who looked just like him") are stashed in footnotes, or scattered amid unsettling scenes from the author's past, growing up in the projects when "teenagers wore automatic weapons like they were sneakers," and dealing "crack to addicts who were killing themselves, collecting the wrinkled bills they got from God knows where, and making sure they got their rocks to smoke."

"Decoded" does not really grapple directly or in detail with several somber episodes in the author's life, like his reported shooting, when he was 12, of his crack-addicted brother (who, according to a recent article in The Guardian, "did not press charges and apologized to his little brother for his addiction"), or his own narrow escape from what an article on Forbes.com has called "a failed attempt on his life" after "a dispute with rival dealers." For that matter, this book — which thanks Dream Hampton, a former editor of the hip-hop magazine The Source, for her help — appears to be a variation on a more straightforward autobiography, written with Ms. Hampton, which Jay-Z decided not to publish several years ago.

Shawn Carter's past would supply the subject matter for Jay-Z's best-known lyrics, and he notes here that when he began writing about his life and the lives of the people around him, "the rhymes helped me twist some sense out of those stories": "flesh and blood became words, ideas, metaphors, fantasies and jokes."

Jay-Z neither romanticizes his days in the street nor apologizes for them, and while it may seem pretentious to supply detailed footnotes to a comical, party-down song like "Big Pimpin'," his annotations to other lyrics are revealing. For instance, of the now ubiquitous "Empire State of

Mind," he says that when he first heard the gorgeous track, his decision was "to dirty it up," to "tell stories of the city's gritty side, to use stories about hustling and getting hustled to add tension to the soaring beauty of the chorus." In doing so, he reminds us that this song, which has virtually replaced "New York, New York" as Gotham's unofficial anthem, contains some remarkably raw references to drug dealing ("Welcome to the melting pot,/Corners where we selling rocks") and promiscuous sex ("The city of sin is a pity on a whim,/Good girls gone bad, the city's filled with them").

In the end, "Decoded" leaves the reader with a keen appreciation of how rap artists have worked myriad variations on a series of familiar themes (hustling, partying and "the most familiar subject in the history of rap — why I'm dope") by putting a street twist on an arsenal of traditional literary devices (hyperbole, double entendres, puns, alliteration and allusions), and how the author himself magically stacks rhymes upon rhymes, mixing and matching metaphors even as he makes unexpected stream-of-consciousness leaps that rework old clichés and play clever aural jokes on the listener ("ruthless" and "roofless," "tears" and "tiers," "sense" and "since").

Just as Jay-Z's eclectic sampling on his records affirms his postmodernist fascination with musical DNA, so this book attests to his love of music and respect for its history, and his debt to his parents' incredible collection of LPs, "stacked to the ceiling in metal milk crates" — soul and R&B, pop and Motown and funk that he would "smuggle" into his own records and give new life to.

"We were kids without fathers, so we found our fathers on wax and on the streets and in history, and in a way, that was a gift," he writes near the end of this provocative, evocative book. "We got to pick and choose the ancestors who would inspire the world we were going to make for ourselves. That was part of the ethos of that time and place, and it got built in to the culture we created. Rap took the remnants of a dying society and created something new. Our fathers were gone, usually because they just bounced, but we took their old records and used them to build something fresh."

# With Arena, Rapper Rewrites Celebrity Investors' Playbook

BY DAVID M. HALBFINGER  |  AUG. 15, 2012

WHEN THE DEVELOPER Bruce Ratner set out to buy the New Jersey Nets and build an arena for them in Brooklyn, he recruited Jay-Z, the hip-hop superstar who grew up in public housing a couple of miles from the site, to join his group of investors.

Mr. Ratner may have thought he was getting little more than a limited partner with a boldface name and a youthful following that could prove useful someday. But Jay-Z's contributions have dwarfed the $1 million he invested nine years ago. His influence on the project has been wildly disproportionate to his ownership stake — a scant one-fifteenth of one percent of the team. And so is the money he stands to make from it.

Now, with the long-delayed Barclays Center arena nearing opening night in September and the Nets bidding in earnest for Brooklyn's loyalties, Jay-Z will perform eight sold-out shows to kick things off. But away from center stage he has put his mark on almost every facet of the enterprise, his partners say.

He helped design the team logos and choose the team's stark black-and-white color scheme, and personally appealed to National Basketball Association officials to drop their objections to it (the N.B.A., according to a person with knowledge of the discussion, thought that African-American athletes did not look good on TV in black, an assertion that a league spokesman adamantly denied). He counseled arena executives on what kind of music to play during games. ("Less Jersey," he urged, pushing niche artists like Santigold over old favorites like Bon Jovi.)

He even coached them on how to screen patrons for weapons without appearing too heavy-handed. ("Be mindful," he advised oracularly, "and be sensitive.")

In the two and a half years since groundbreaking, as taxi-roof advertisements promised "All access to Jay-Z," and sponsorship salespeople trumpeted how "hip and cool" he and his wife, Beyoncé, would make the arena, he and the Nets have effectively written a new playbook for how to deploy a strategic celebrity investor.

If it has been done elsewhere — see Usher with the Cleveland Cavaliers, Will Smith with the Philadelphia 76ers, and Jennifer Lopez and Marc Anthony with the Miami Dolphins — no team has come close to making as much out of a famous part-owner.

And none of the dozens of other current and former part-owners of the team have played so public a role — not even Mary Higgins Clark, the best-selling author, though she read to children at a Nets literacy event.

"He is it," Mr. Ratner, the developer, said in an interview. "He is us. He is how people are going to see that place."

As much as his partners, including Mikhail D. Prokhorov, the Russian billionaire who bought 80 percent of the team in 2009, are getting out of him, Jay-Z, whose real name is Shawn Carter, is benefiting handsomely, too, beginning with free use of one of 11 exclusive "Vault" suites, for which paying customers are charged $550,000 a year.

Suite owners will have access to a Champagne bar serving Armand de Brignac, an expensive bubbly that Mr. Carter promotes and in which he holds a financial interest, according to a biography by a writer for Forbes. The arena will contain a 40/40 Club, an iteration of his sports-bar-style nightclub chain. There will be a Rocawear store, selling his clothing line, on the arena's exterior. Even the advertising agency used by the Nets, Translation, is half-owned by Mr. Carter.

There is also an important intangible asset, particularly for a rapper: the bragging rights that Mr. Carter has enjoyed as a part-owner since Mr. Ratner's group paid $300 million to acquire the Nets. His slender stake was enough for Mr. Carter to thump his chest in his lyrics, promising to "bring you some Nets."

Mr. Carter has capitalized further on his Nets investment by extending the Jay-Z brand into endorsement deals normally reserved for elite athletes. He stars, wearing a Nets cap, in a Budweiser TV commercial that was broadcast during the Olympic Games. And he was named executive producer of the basketball video game, "NBA 2K13."

All told, he has achieved a remarkable feat of leverage with his tiny sliver of the team, which was reduced from one-third to one-fifteenth of a percent upon Mr. Prokhorov's purchase of the Nets, according to people aware of the deal terms. (Mr. Carter, who declined to be interviewed for this article, retains a slightly larger sliver of the arena itself — just under a fifth of a percent.)

As if to slam that point home, when the Nets placed a 222-foot-tall billboard near Madison Square Garden depicting Mr. Carter and Mr. Prokhorov as their "blueprint for greatness," the two were shown at the same size, with Mr. Carter up front.

Mr. Ratner said he was seeking both sizzle and "credibility — which we needed badly," when he first approached several other celebrities in 2003 about helping him acquire the team. Then he was introduced to Mr. Carter by Drew Katz, the son of one of the Nets' principal owners, after Jason Kidd, then the Nets' marquee point guard, suggested that Mr. Carter buy the team.

Mr. Carter's credibility was indisputable: a product of the Marcy Houses, he had an early career as a drug dealer (and kept a "stash spot" two blocks from the arena site, according to one of his songs) before becoming one of the most successful rap artists of all time. He had also shown talent as a businessman, creating his own record label and what soon became a wide range of other business ventures.

Mr. Ratner was wary. He often says he overcame his concerns about Mr. Carter's more offensive lyrics — celebrating gangster culture and denigrating women — only after learning there were cleaned-up "radio versions" of the songs, too. And Mr. Carter, he said, appeared nervous about having to meet with David Stern, the N.B.A. commissioner, who asked him to discuss his guilty plea to stabbing a record producer in 1999. (Mr. Carter described the incident, for which he received three years' probation, as a symptom of "the world I lived in once," Mr. Ratner recalled.)

Mr. Carter's involvement frustrated opponents of Mr. Ratner's development plans in Brooklyn who saw the arena and proposed residential and office towers as a subsidized land grab that could ruin the neighborhood. They complained that residents who might have been wary of Mr. Ratner's promises to create jobs, nonetheless trusted Jay-Z, who invoked his roots and insisted he could never support "anything that's against the people."

"Bringing in someone who grew up in public housing, with a rags-to-riches story, who could identify with Brooklyn and African-Americans, that was slick," said City Councilwoman Letitia James, a critic of the project. Mr. Ratner played down Mr. Carter's importance in overcoming opposition. "Had Jay-Z not come along," he said, "we'd still have an arena."

In the early years, as the Nets made playoff runs, Mr. Carter freely associated himself with the team, attending games and suggesting how to entertain V.I.P.'s in style, said Brett Yormark, chief executive of the Nets. "He and I would talk about how we could use New Jersey as a lab experiment for Brooklyn," he said.

He also made himself useful to the basketball staff, persuading Shareef Abdur-Rahim of the Portland Trail Blazers to accept a 2005 trade to the Nets (an injury scuttled the deal) and giving Vince Carter a pep talk after he played poorly in two playoff games in 2007 (he responded with 37 points in the next game).

But the rap star pulled back from the Nets as their fortunes faded and they failed to make the playoffs after the 2007-8 season. "He's very brand-conscious," a Nets official said.

It was only after the Barclays Center had cleared all hurdles in December 2009 that Mr. Carter unabashedly stepped forward. He courted LeBron James on behalf of the Nets in 2010 and pursued Carmelo Anthony a year later. And when the Nets' newest star, Deron Williams, needed advice on where to buy a home, Mr. Carter told him to call.

Aaron Goodwin, an agent who has represented many young players who became N.B.A. stars, said Mr. Carter's involvement had improved the image of the Nets in athletes' eyes. "They're going to take the phone call now," he said. "They're going to take the flight in. They're going to listen. In years past, the Nets wouldn't have gotten that. But now they're in the game." Mr. Yormark said Mr. Carter was not receiving a fee for his advice or any special deals for his businesses. Yet he has attended both quarterly meetings of the arena's board of directors, sitting to Mr. Ratner's right, and keeps in frequent touch by phone and e-mail with Mr. Yormark.

During the Nets' free-agency deal making this summer — obtaining Joe Johnson and re-signing Mr. Williams, among others, in hopes of improving upon their 22-44 record last season — Mr. Yormark received a call from Mr. Carter, who was following the team's moves on television. "He said he was watching ESPN," Mr. Yormark said, "and the size of our logo was too big, because the word Brooklyn was getting cut off on the ticker at the bottom of the screen. He said, 'Call ESPN and get them to fix it.' And he was right. And then they fixed it."

When Mr. Yormark next sat down for a meeting with Mr. Carter, he recalled, the rap star reminded him of this, saying: "Brett, I'm watching. And every detail matters."

# The House That Hova Built

BY ZADIE SMITH | SEPT. 6, 2012

IT'S DIFFICULT TO KNOW what to ask a rapper. It's not unlike the difficulty (I imagine) of being a rapper. Whatever you say must be considered from at least three angles, and it's an awkward triangulation. In one corner you have your hard-core hip-hop heads; the type for whom the true Jay-Z will forever be that gifted 25-year-old with rapid-fire flow, trading verses with the visionary teenager Big L — "I'm so ahead of my time, my parents haven't met yet!" — on a "rare" (easily dug up on YouTube) seven-minute freestyle from 1995. Meanwhile, over here stands the pop-rap fan. She loves the Jiggaman with his passion for the Empire State Building and bold claims to "Run This Town." Finally, in the crowded third corner, stand the many people who feel rap is not music at all but rather a form of social problem. They have only one question to ask a rapper, and it concerns his choice of vocabulary. (Years pass. The question never changes.) How to speak to these audiences simultaneously? Anyway: I'm at a little table in a homey Italian restaurant on Mulberry Street waiting for Mr. Shawn Carter, who has perfected the art of triangulation. It's where he likes to eat his chicken parms.

He's not late. He's dressed like a kid, in cap and jeans, if he said he was 30 you wouldn't doubt him. (He's 42.) He's overwhelmingly familiar, which is of course a function of his fame — rap superstar, husband of Beyoncé, minority owner of the Nets, whose new home, the Barclays Center in Brooklyn, will open this month — but also of the fact he's been speaking into our ears for so long. No one stares. The self-proclaimed "greatest rapper alive" is treated like a piece of the furniture. Ah, but there's always one: a preppy white guy discreetly operating his iPhone's reverse-camera function. It's an old hustle; it makes Jay chuckle: "They think they're the first one who's ever come up with that concept."

He likes to order for people. Apparently I look like the fish-sandwich type. Asked if he thinks this is a good time for hip-hop, he enthuses about how inclusive hip-hop is: "It provided a gateway to conversations that normally would not be had." And now that rap's reached this unprecedented level of cultural acceptance, maybe we're finally free to celebrate the form without needing to continually defend it. *Say that I'm foolish I only talk about jewels/Do you fools listen to music or do you just skim through it?* He's not so sure: "It's funny how you can say things like that in plain English and then people still do it." He is mildly disappointed that after publishing "Decoded," his 2010 memoir, people still ask the same old questions. The flippancy annoys him, the ease with which some still dismiss rap as "something that's just this bad language, or guys who degrade women, and they don't realize the poetry and the art." This is perhaps one downside to having the "flow of the century."

With Tupac, you can hear the effort, the artistry. And Biggie's words first had to struggle free of the sheer bulk of the man himself. When Jay raps, it pours right into your ear like water from a tap.

The fish sandwich arrives. Conversation turns to the schoolboy who was shot to death, Trayvon Martin — "It's really heartbreaking, that that still can happen in this day and age" — and, soon after, to Obama: "I've said the election of Obama has made the hustler less relevant." When he first made this point, "People took it in a way that I was almost dismissing what I am. And I was like: no, it's a good thing!" He didn't have Obama growing up, only the local hustler. "No one came to our neighborhoods, with stand-up jobs, and showed us there's a different way. Maybe had I seen different role models, maybe I'd've turned on to that." Difficult to keep these two Americas in your mind. Imagine living it — within one lifetime!

In "Decoded," Jay-Z writes that "rap is built to handle contradictions," and Hova, as he is nicknamed, is as contradictory as they come. Partly because he's a generalist. Biggie had better boasts, Tupac dropped more knowledge, Eminem is — as "Renegade" demonstrated — more formally dexterous. But Hova's the all-rounder. His albums are showrooms of hip-hop, displaying the various possibilities of the form. The persona is cool, calm, almost frustratingly self-controlled: "Yeah, 50 Cent told me that one time. He said: 'You got me looking like Barksdale' " — the hot-blooded drug kingpin from HBO's "The Wire" — "and you get to be Stringer Bell!" — Barksdale's levelheaded partner. The rapper Memphis Bleek, who has known Jay-Z since Bleek himself was 14, confirms this impression: "He had a sense of calm way before music. This was Jay's plan from day one: to take over. I guess that's why he smiles and is so calm, 'cause he did exactly what he planned in the '90s." And now, by virtue of being 42 and not dead, he can claim his own unique selling proposition: he's an artist as old as his art form. The two have grown up together.

Jay-Z, like rap itself, started out pyrotechnical. Extremely fast, stacked, dense. But time passed and his flow got slower, opened up. Why? "I didn't have enough life experience, so what I was doing was more technical. I was trying to impress technically. To do things that other people cannot do. Like, you can't do this" — insert beat-box and simultaneous freestyle here — "you just can't do that." Nope. Can't even think of a notation to demonstrate what he just did. Jay-Z in technician mode is human voice as pure syncopation. On a track like "I Can't Get With That," from 1994, the manifest content of the music is never really the words themselves; it's the rhythm they create. And if you don't care about beats, he says, "You've missed the whole point."

Plenty did, hearing only a young black man, boasting. *I got watches I ain't seen in months/Apartment at the Trump I only slept in once.*

But asking why rappers always talk about their stuff is like asking why Milton is forever listing the attributes of heavenly armies. Because boasting is a formal condition of the epic form. And those taught that they deserve nothing rightly enjoy it when they succeed in terms the culture understands. Then something changed: "As I started getting life experiences, I realized my power was in conveying emotions that people felt." He compared himself to a comedian whose jokes trigger this reaction: "Yo, that's so true." He started storytelling — people were mesmerized. "Friend or Foe" (1996), which concerns a confrontation between two hustlers, is rap in its masterful, full-blown, narrative form. Not just a monologue, but a story, complete with dialogue, scene setting, characterization. Within its comic flow and light touch — free from the relentless sincerity of Tupac — you can hear the seeds of 50, Lil Wayne, Eminem, so many others. "That was the first one where it was so obvious," Jay noted. He said the song represented an important turning point, the moment when he "realized I was doing it."

At times he restricts himself formally, like the Oulipo, that experimental French literary group of the 1960s. In the song "22 Two's," from 1996, we get 22 delicious plays on the words "too" and "two."

Ten years later, the sequel, "44 Fours," has the same conceit, stepped up a gear. "Like, you know, close the walls in a bit smaller." Can he explain why? "I think the reason I still make music is because of the challenge." He doesn't believe in relying solely on one's natural gifts. And when it comes to talent, "You just never know — there is no gauge. You don't see when it's empty."

In the years since his masterpiece "Reasonable Doubt," the rapper has often been accused of running on empty, too distant now from what once made him real. In "Decoded," he answers existentially: "How distant is the story of your own life ever going to be?" In the lyrics, practically:

*Life stories told through rap/Niggas actin' like I sold you crack/ Like I told you sell drugs, no, Hov' did that/So hopefully you won't have to go through that.* But can't a rapper insist, like other artists, on a fictional reality, in which he is somehow still on the corner, despite occupying the penthouse suite? *Out hustlin', same clothes for days/I'll never change, I'm too stuck in my ways.* Can't he still rep his block? For Jay-Z, pride in the block has been essential and he recognized rap's role in taking "that embarrassment off of you. The first time people were saying: I come from here — and it's O.K." He quotes Mobb Deep: "No matter how much money I get, I'm staying in the projects!" But here, too, he sees change: "Before, if you didn't have that authenticity, your career could be over. Vanilla Ice said he got stabbed or something, they found out he was lying, he was finished." I suggested to him that many readers of this newspaper would find it bizarre that the reputation of the rapper Rick Ross was damaged when it was revealed a few years ago that he was, at one time, a prison guard. "But again," Jay says, "I think hip-hop has moved away from that place of every-thing has to be authentic. Kids are growing up very differently now."

Sure are. Odd Future. Waka Flocka Flame. Chief Keef. Returning to what appear to be the basic building blocks of rap: shock tactics, obscenity, perversely simplistic language. After the sophistication of Rakim, Q-Tip, Nas, Lupe Fiasco, Kanye West and Jay himself, are we back on the corner again? "Yeah, but Tupac was an angel compared to these artists!" He shakes his head, apparently amused at himself. And it's true: listening to a Tupac record these days feels like listening to a pleasant slice of Sinatra. But Jay-Z does not suffer from nostalgia. He loves Odd Future and their punk rock vibe. He sees their anger as a general "aversion to corporate America," particularly as far as it has despoiled the planet. "People have a real aversion to what people in power did to the country. So they're just lashing out, like: 'This is the son that you made. Look at your son. Look at what you've done.'"

But surely another thing they're reacting against, in the Harold Bloom "anxiety of influence" sense, is the gleaming $460 million mon-ument of Hova himself.

Years ago, Martin Amis wrote a funny story, "Career Move," in which the screenwriters live like poets, starving in garrets, while the poets chillax poolside, fax their verses to agents in Los Angeles and earn millions off a sonnet. Last year's "Watch the Throne," a collab-oration with Kanye, concerns the coming to pass of that alternative reality. *Hundred stack/How you get it?* Jay-Z asks Kanye on "Gotta Have It." The answer seems totally improbable, and yet it's the truth: Layin' raps on tracks! Fortunes made from rhyming verse. Which is what makes "Watch the Throne" interesting: it fully expresses black America's present contradictions. *It's a celebration of black excellence/ Black tie, black Maybachs/Black excellence, opulence, decadence.* But it's also a bitter accounting of the losses in a long and unfinished war.

Kanye raps: *I feel the pain in my city wherever I go/314 soldiers died in Iraq/509 died in Chicago.* Written by a couple of millionaire businessmen on the fly ("Like 'New Day,' Kanye told me that — the actual rap — last year at the Met Ball, in my ear at dinner"), it really shouldn't be as good as it is. But somehow their brotherly rivalry creates real energy despite the mammoth production. And in one vital way the process of making it was unusually intimate: "Most people nowadays — because of technology — send music back and forth." But this was just two men "sitting in a room, and really talking about this." At its most sublime — the ridiculously enjoyable "Niggas in Paris" — you feel a strong pull in both men toward sheer abandon, pure celebration. Didn't we earn this? Can't we sit back and enjoy it? It's a song that doesn't want to be responsible, or to be asked the old, painful questions. Who cares if they're keeping it real? Or even making sense? Check that beat! Then there's that word. "It's a lot of pain and a lot of hurt and a lot of things going on beyond, beneath that." He offers an analogy: "If your kid was acting up, you'd be like, 'What is wrong with you?' If they have a bellyache — 'Oh, you ate all the cotton candy.' You'd make these comparisons, you'd see a link. You'd psychoanalyze the situation."

Rappers use language as a form of asymmetrical warfare. How else to explain George W. Bush's extraordinary contention that a line spoken by a rapper — "George Bush doesn't care about black people" — was "one of the most disgusting moments in my presidency"? But there have always been these people for whom rap language is more scandalous than the urban deprivation rap describes. On "Who Gon Stop Me," Jay-Z asks that we "please pardon all the curses" because "when you're growing up worthless," well, things come out that way. Black hurt, black self-esteem. It's the contradictory pull of the "cipher," rap terminology for the circle that forms around the kind of freestyling kid Jay-Z once was. What a word! Cipher (noun): 1. A secret or disguised way of writing; a code. 2. A key to such a code. 3. A person or thing of no importance. "Watch the Throne" celebrates two men's escape from that circle of negation. It paints the world black: black bar mitzvahs, black cars, paintings of black girls in the MoMA, all black everything, as if it might be possible in a single album to peel back thousands of years of negative connotation. Black no longer the shadow or the reverse or the opposite of something but now the thing itself. But living this fantasy proves problematic: *Only spot a few blacks the higher I go/What's up to Will? Shout-out to O/That ain't enough, we gon' need a million more/ Kick in the door, Biggie flow/I'm all dressed up with nowhere to go. You're 1 percent of the 1 percent. So what now? Power to the people, when you see me, see you!* But that just won't do. It's Jay-Z who's in Paris, after all, not the kids in the Marcy Houses, the housing project in Brooklyn where he grew up. Jay-Z knows this. He gets a little agitated when the subject of Zuccotti Park comes up: "What's the thing on the wall, what are you fighting for?" He says he told Russell Simmons, the rap mogul, the same: "I'm not going to a park and picnic, I have no idea what to do, I don't know what the fight is about. What do we want, do you know?"

Jay-Z likes clarity: "I think all those things need to really declare themselves a bit more clearly. Because when you just say that 'the 1 percent is that,' that's not true. Yeah, the 1 percent that's robbing people, and deceiving people, these fixed mortgages and all these things, and then taking their home away from them, that's criminal, that's bad. Not being an entrepreneur. This is free enterprise. This is what America is built on."

It's so weird watching rappers becoming elder statesmen. I'm out for presidents to represent me. Well, now they do — and not only on dollar bills. Heavy responsibility lands on the shoulders of these unacknowledged legislators whose poetry is only, after all, four decades young. Jay-Z's ready for it. He has his admirable Shawn Carter Scholarship Foundation, putting disadvantaged kids through college. He's spoken in support of gay rights. He's curating music festivals and investing in environmental technologies. This October, his beloved Nets take up residence in their new home — the Barclays Center in Brooklyn. And he has some canny, forward-looking political instincts: "I was speaking to my friend James, who's from London, we were talking about something else, I just stopped and I was like, 'What's going to happen in London?' This was maybe a month before the riots. He was like, 'What?' I said: 'The culture of black people there, they're not participating in changing the direction of the country. What's gonna happen there?' He actually called me when it blew up, he was like, 'You know, I didn't really understand your question, or the timing of it, until now.' "

But still I think "conscious" rap fans hope for something more from him; to see, perhaps, a final severing of this link, in hip-hop, between material riches and true freedom. (Though why we should expect rappers to do this ahead of the rest of America isn't clear.) It would take real forward thinking. Of his own ambitions for the future, he says: "I don't want to do anything that isn't true." Maybe the next horizon will stretch beyond philanthropy and Maybach collections.

Meanwhile, back in the rank and file, you still hear the old cry go up: Hip-hop is dead! Which really means that our version of it (the one we knew in our youth) has passed. But nothing could be duller than a '90s hip-hop bore. Lil Wayne? Give me Ol' Dirty Bastard. Nicki Minaj? Please. Foxy Brown. Odd Future? WU TANG CLAN 4EVAH. Listening to Jay-Z — still so flexible and enthusiastic, ears wide open — you realize you're like one of these people who believes jazz died with Dizzy. The check comes. You will be unsurprised to hear the Jiggaman paid. At the last minute, I remembered to ask after his family, "Oh, my family's amazing." And the baby? "She's four months." *Marcy raised me, and whether right or wrong/Streets gave me all I write in the song.* But what will TriBeCa give Blue? "I actually thought about that more before she was born. Once she got here I've been in shock until maybe last week?" Her childhood won't be like his, and this fact he takes in his stride. "We would fight each other. My brother would beat me up," he says, but it was all in preparation for the outside. "I was going to have to fight, I was going to have to go through some things, and they were preparing me." He smiles: "She doesn't have to be tough. She has to love herself, she has to know who she is, she has to be respectful, and be a moral person." It's a new day.

# Jay-Z Is Rhyming Picasso and Rothko

BY GUY TREBAY | JULY 12, 2013

"I HAVE NO IDEA why I'm here," the artist Marilyn Minter said, as she sat in a temporary V.I.P. room at the Pace Gallery in Chelsea on a steamy Wednesday. "I'm just a fame whore."

Ms. Minter was one of hundreds of fans and art-world types — Kalup Linzy; Lawrence Weiner; Andres Serrano; George Condo; Yvonne Force Villareal; Lisa Phillips, the director of the New Museum; and Agnes Gund, MoMA's president emerita — invited to take part in a live filming of Jay-Z's music video for "Picasso Baby," the art-centric song off his new album, "Magna Carta... Holy Grail."

The rap marathon was inspired by the performance artist Marina Abramovic's 2010 MoMA exhibition, "The Artist Is Present," said the art dealer Jeanne Greenberg Rohatyn, who is Jay-Z's art adviser and was a host of the event along with the film director Mark Romanek. "Jay has been wanting to do something durational for some time."

The video shoot added a welcome frisson to Chelsea as the dozy season hit its annual doldrums. And it livened up a corner of the Web, where the topic of art-world fame whores racing to sell out can be counted on to set the thumb-tappers in motion.

Stephanie Theodore, a Bushwick gallery owner, tweeted a wry suggestion that the Chinese dissident artist Ai Weiwei divorce his wife, marry Ms. Abramovic and form a megacult. Why not invite James Franco, the art blog Hyperallergic added, and make it an unholy threesome?

At a mere six hours, the taping was a water-cooler break by the usual standards of Ms. Abramovic, who during the run of "The Artist Is Present," spent the equivalent of 30 full days sitting immobile in the museum atrium, while spectators took turns sitting opposite her. Still, as Mr. Linzy, a performance artist, said, "It's epic."

Jay-Z greets art-world guests before a taping of the music video of his song "Picasso Baby" at the Pace Gallery in Chelsea.

Dressed for the performance not in the Tom Ford suits he favors, but a pair of black jeans, white sneakers, a white short-sleeve shirt, a heavy gold chain, a gumball-size pinkie ring and a wristwatch from his collection of six-figure timepieces, Jay-Z rapped from a platform facing a bench reminiscent of the set of Ms. Abramovic's original artwork.

Like Ms. Abramovic, he was a mesmeric presence, shifting spectators around as though they were iron filings drawn by a magnet. With his usual braggadocio, Jay-Z rapped lyrics like: "I want a Picasso, in my casa ... I wanna Rothko, no I wanna brothel," and "What's it gonna take for me to go, For y'all to see I'm the modern-day Pablo Picasso baby."

He reminded his listeners that, like most every self-respecting millionaire mogul these days, he is an avid collector of contemporary art, although he alone turns the pursuit to his singular ends in lyrics that knowingly name-check everyone from Jeff Koons to Jean-Michel Basquiat.

In "Picasso Baby," Jay-Z's grab bag of references includes Mr. Condo, Art Basel Miami Beach, Francis Bacon, the Museum of Modern Art, the Tate Modern and Andy Warhol. He cites Basquiat twice, preening his insider knowledge by lyrically incorporating both the artist's given name and Samo, his original graffiti tag.

To some spectators, it was particularly bracing to watch a hip-hop god colonize a white cube world that must once have seemed as distant as Mars from the Marcy Houses in Brooklyn, the projects where Jay-Z grew up (and where he was known by his given name, Shawn Carter). "For a young black man in America to be on his level of success and rapping about art, and not what he's wearing, is the coolest thing," the artist Mickalene Thomas said.

"People have to realize he's referencing artists who have been shape-shifters in themselves," she added. "They have to know that a young person hearing him saying 'I am Picasso,' is going to look up Picasso."

Ms. Minter, whose lush photorealist paintings comment on glamour and decadence, said, "Jay-Z speaks to the times we live in."

An Mr. Weiner, an austere conceptualist, added, "Jay-Z speaks with the times he lives in."

Unquestionably, Jay-Z manipulates our credulous times as deftly as he did a crowd that also included Judd Apatow, the designer Cynthia Rowley, Alan Cumming, Adam Driver and the artist Marcel Dzama, who came to the filming wearing a cow costume he constructed for a recent video.

"It's great how he has really recreated the whole MoMA feel," Mr. Dzama said. And it helped that Ms. Abramovic herself was on hand, arriving theatrically an hour into the event and emerging from a stretch S.U.V. with a turbaned chauffeur. Wearing one of the floor-length black dresses that a friend, the Givenchy designer Riccardo Tisci, creates for her, Ms. Abramovic stepped from the vehicle and glided into the gallery with the hypnotic gravity of some loopy space priestess from a sci-fi kitsch classic of the '50s.

Cameras in her wake, she parted the crowd — "Queen of Outer Space" meets the hip-hop monarch — crossing the gallery to mount a low platform, where she and Jay-Z engaged in a pas de deux sure to go down as among the oddest moments in the annals of performance art.

Two minutes later, the dance had already been posted to Vine and gone art-world viral. "OK the video in Infinite Jest that entertains you to death has finally come and it is the Vine of Jay-Z & Marina Abramovic," wrote @LindsayZoladz. "R.I.P. US ALL."

Don't close the coffin lid quite yet.

Like Ms. Abramovic, whose stare-downs at MoMA left so many participants in tears that it inspired the blog "Marina Abramovic Made Me Cry," the Jay-Z video was too sincere, even in its cynicism, to be all bad.

To a large extent, that was owed to the hip-hop artist's way with the crowd, both mellow and collaborative. When a generator cut out, taking with it the background music, Jay-Z called out: "Anyone got unusual talents? Anyone can do something awesome?" He then invited a ballet dancer to perform some pirouettes; the performance artist Jacolby Satterwhite to show off his vogueing; and Kiah Victoria, a music student, to blow the roof off the gallery with her a cappella rendition of a torch song.

"I just love the way Jay-Z riffs on what Marina did," said Roselee Goldberg, the performance art historian and founder of Performa.

That the boo-birds on Twitter failed to share the love will doubtless help Jay-Z's cause or, anyway, his record sales. The shock and peril that once characterized much performance art had been co-opted by a marketing wizard, turned, as the bloggers carped, into a tool of aesthetic predictability.

Here it seems proper to resuscitate both Andy Warhol's famous observation that "being good in business is the most fascinating kind of art," and to paraphrase an aphorism often attributed to the actual Picasso: mediocre artists borrow, great artists steal.

# Jay Z and Beyoncé: Activism Gone Vocal

BY JON CARAMANICA  |  JULY 8, 2016

IN 2012, the singer, actor and civil rights leader Harry Belafonte indicted, among others, Jay Z and Beyoncé as being part of a generation of black artists who have "turned their back on social responsibility." It was a rare public upbraiding for a couple who had so effectively shifted American pop culture, but whose work for social change was primarily rooted in what they accomplished on record, not off.

Four years later, the social landscape has shifted: Politics have moved from the implicit to the explicit, and culture is following in tow, helped in no small part by Jay Z and Beyoncé, who are increasingly using their outsize platform as a tool of social agitation. In the wake of the police killings of Philando Castile and Alton Sterling this week — but before news broke of the shooting deaths of five police officers in Dallas — both released bold statements, weaving together their activism and their art.

Beyoncé posted a staunch statement of frustration on her website. "These robberies of lives make us feel helpless and hopeless," she wrote, "but we have to believe that we are fighting for the rights of the next generation, for the next young men and women who believe in good." At her concert in Glasgow on Thursday night, she sang her rousing political anthem "Freedom" a cappella in front of a screen bearing the names of police brutality victims.

Late Thursday night, on his streaming service, Tidal, Jay Z released "Spiritual," a song motivated by anger — and exhaustion — about police brutality, in which he repeats the refrain "Just a boy from the 'hood that/Got my hands in the air/In despair, don't shoot."

Mr. Belafonte's critique came just a few months after the birth of Blue Ivy, Jay Z and Beyoncé's daughter. That their newly outward focus on social justice coincides with their years raising her isn't a

After the police killings of Philando Castile and Alton Sterling this week, Jay Z has released a song on his streaming service about police brutality.

surprise — who wants to make the world a better place more than a parent? A child gives purpose.

And hearing Jay Z rap about his daughter in recent years, in ways both ecstatic and restless, has been the main pleasure of what's almost certainly the twilight of his rapping career.

In 2013, on the song "Jay Z Blue," he presented himself completely free of bravado. He detailed his fears — Can someone who was never properly fathered become a worthy father? Can a parent ever truly protect a child? — and foreshadowed the marital tensions that his wife, Beyoncé, would later mine so effectively on her 2016 album, "Lemonade."

All the same themes are there on the frenzied, fragmented "Spiritual." But this time, it's not domestic strife threatening Blue's calm, it's what's happening in the rest of the world. What unnerves Jay Z is that you can improve your own behavior, but you can't control anyone else's: He can't fix persistent police violence against black bodies.

*I'm smack dab*
*In a hurricane of emotions*
*Can't even raise my little daughter, my little Carter*
*We call her Blue 'cause it's sad that*
*How can I be a dad that, I never had that*
*Shattered in a million pieces, where the glass at*
*I need a drink, shrink or something*
*I need an angelic voice to sing something*
*Bless my soul, extend your arms, I'm cold*
*Hold me for a half-hour 'til I'm whole*

In a note that accompanied the release of "Spiritual," Jay Z said he wrote the song some time ago, before the killing of Michael Brown in Ferguson, Mo., in 2014 galvanized the Black Lives Matter movement. "I'm hurt that I knew his death wouldn't be the last," he wrote. "I'm saddened and disappointed in THIS America — we should be further along. WE ARE NOT."

In 2016, Jay Z is less an essential figure in contemporary hip-hop than an exemplar of the possibilities a life in the genre can afford. But as "Spiritual" makes plain, even he can feel helpless: "This is tougher than any gun that I raised/Any crack that I blazed, that was nothing."

Jay Z's emergence as an activist, from sub rosa to out in the open, has been the quiet counterpoint to his very public entrepreneurship in recent years. He helped Brooklyn Nets players secure "I Can't Breathe" T-shirts to wear following the police killing of Eric Garner. He and Beyoncé reportedly contributed money to bail out arrested Baltimore and Ferguson protesters. He announced that he would funnel money to a variety of social justice groups from proceeds raised in a charity concert given by Tidal last year.

Beyoncé's activism has been more closely tied to her art. Early this year, she released "Formation," on which she sang intensely about black beauty and cultural pride. In the video, a dancing black boy induces a row of armed officers to raise their hands in surrender, and Beyoncé herself is draped atop a police cruiser as it sinks into the water. Her vigorous Super Bowl halftime show performance of the song included nods to the Black Panthers; it was the most widely seen act of political art in recent memory.

Of course, it inspired protests. At concerts on her current "Formation" tour, she sells a T-shirt that reads "Boycott Beyoncé" — a taunt and a wink.

For Jay Z and Beyoncé, speaking loudly has become the new normal. As much as parenting is love, warmth, astonishment and joy, it is also unease, uncertainty, humility, fear. Jay Z and Beyoncé are confronting those feelings head-on — it's their way of building a bridge to the past and securing a road for the future.

# Jay-Z Revels in the Catharsis of Confession on '4:44'

ALBUM REVIEW | BY JON CARAMANICA | JULY 2, 2017

WHEN RAPPER SELF-MYTHOLOGIZING was in its infancy, Jay-Z was its most faithful student. He absorbed the art of the boast, and built on that to create one of pop's most fascinating characters: the street-corner hustler turned multimillionaire, slick and unbothered. Complex emotions often formed the foundation of his tales of ascendancy, but his greatest talent was making his path seem smooth and inevitable. No matter how high the stakes, he remained cold as ice.

When you are on top, or racing there, this is an unimpeachable approach. But when you've been reigning for a while, it can come to seem despotic, ungenerous, false. When your equally famous wife lays waste to that manicured image with an album full of personal, musical and political fire, continuing with the old way of doing things is not an option. Evolve or disappear. Find new life or accept death.

As an elder statesman — recently the first rapper to be enshrined in the Songwriters Hall of Fame — Jay-Z would have been forgiven for tapping out and letting silence be a kind of victory. Only extreme emotional-spiritual catharsis or extreme stripped-down intimacy would make for a worthwhile comeback.

On the confidently vulnerable "4:44," his 13th studio album and first in four years, he has chosen both. Viewed from different angles, "4:44" (Roc Nation) is a long-simmering, eyes-downcast confession; a relaxing of muscles that have been tense for decades; the return of a rule-rewriting mastermind as a moralist and occasional scold; a marketing ploy intended to bolster two second-tier businesses, the streaming service Tidal and the phone company Sprint. (For now, at least, you need one or both to listen to the album, without seeking out a bootleg.)

Jay-Z's 13th studio album, "4:44," is candid and raw, and doesn't try to compete with the sounds of today's up-and-coming rappers.

It is also the first Jay-Z album in a decade that doesn't pretend to be competing in the present moment. It is the sound of a 47-year-old aesthete working at his own pace, dismantling his facade and reminding himself of all the natural poignancy that the bluster has been obscuring.

"I fall short of what I say I'm all about," he says on the title track, his apology to his wife, Beyoncé, for the indiscretions that led her to publicly shame him. The album begins with "Kill Jay Z," an extended tsk-tsk to himself. "You can't heal what you never reveal," he raps. "You know you owe the truth/To all the youth that fell in love with Jay-Z."

And so the confessions, or certainly what appear to be confessions, pour out.

Yes, he cheated on Beyoncé (the title track, among others); yes, he's tried therapy ("Smile"); yes, he stabbed the executive Lance Rivera back in 1999 ("Kill Jay Z"); yes, his father's side of the family was darkened by abuse ("Legacy"); yes, his mother is gay, and was in the closet for decades ("Smile"); yes, he's fed up with Kanye West's scattershot antics ("Kill Jay Z," among others).

That is, assuming everything here is true, and not just the second installment of a multi-album musicanovela in which he and his wife portray bitter lovers bound together by fate, fame and farce.

Jay-Z has been this candid before, but never quite this naked. These aren't stories told to fortify a magisterial image but rather the exhale of a long-held breath.

In some plain narrative ways, "4:44" is a companion piece to Beyoncé's "Lemonade." On the title track, Jay-Z is vividly self-critical: "I've seen the innocence leave your eyes/I still mourn this death," he tells his wife.

But the two albums also share an emphasis on black self-sufficiency — on "Lemonade," the argument was sociopolitical; here, it's largely financial. On "The Story of O. J.," Jay-Z raps about cross-generational wealth — passing his art collection down to his children — with the same fervor and lyrical gambit he once used to rap about amassing personal wealth (on "U Don't Know," in 2001). The kingpin is now just a vessel for tomorrow's dreams.

The whole of "4:44" was produced by No I.D., who produced much of Common's essential work, and who prepared a sample-driven, skin-and-bones, slightly greasy palette for Jay-Z to rap over. Most of the album hovers between 80-90 beats per minute, but feels slower, thanks to the way No I.D. forgoes crispness in favor of beats that slur, drag and bleed. There's also patina on the vocals. Nothing gleams — not the beats, not the words, not the feelings.

The relative sparseness acts as suction: There are barely any distractions. It's almost like an unplugged album, a kind of platonic raw course of rapper, producer, sample and beat. In places, it suggests a bare-bones counterpoint to one of Jay-Z's masterworks, "The Blueprint," from 2001, which relied on the steroidal soul-informed production of Mr. West and Just Blaze to echo Jay-Z at his most conceited.

Ornamentation has long served Jay-Z well, so the lack of glamour here is striking. Part of the thrill of listening to him has been how lustrously he paints the unattainable. That underneath it all is a man full of regret is both obvious and, at times, a bit deflating. When he laments not investing in the now-redeveloped Brooklyn neighborhood Dumbo on "The Story of O. J.," it's not clever, just a gripe. And one delivered without much flair.

The qualities that made Jay-Z one of rap's true savants were his sly wit and the way he threaded himself into the production — few rappers have found more creative ways to disperse their syllables, and sounded tougher and less fatigued while doing it. The Jay-Z of "4:44" isn't quite there. He's evolved from dazzling taunts to ruminations that are sometimes snappy and sometimes lumpy. When snappy, though, they're exhilarating, like the opening of "Caught Their Eyes," which has the snarl Jay-Z arrived with fully formed on his 1996 debut album, "Reasonable Doubt": "I survived reading guys like you/I'm surprised y'all think y'all can disguise y'all truths."

At this stage of his career, though, keeping up with the Migos would be a fool's task. He's a veteran, and it shows: On three songs, he's baffled about how the younger generation uses Instagram as a tool of exaggerated street theater. And while the Jay-Z of 10 years ago would have been improvising his way through Young Thug and Playboi Carti anti-flows both as an exercise in hubris and also competitive vim, there's none of that here.

Rather, he makes a strong case for artistically aging by drilling down to core principles. As albums of late-career reckoning go, "4:44" isn't quite Gaye or Sinatra or Cash, but it's on the path. Uncomfortable truths unearthed, demons shouted down, process refined — even when everything melts away, you can still be ice-cold.

# Jay-Z and the Politics of Rapping in Middle Age

BY WESLEY MORRIS | JULY 19, 2017

"OLD SCHOOL" still has some currency in hip-hop. It nods to forebears, styles and history. "Old" is a different story. "Old" means you're past your prime. It means you have nothing new to say — and even if you did, who would want to listen? "Old" means maybe you know what's new, but you want to do it the way you've always done it. So "old" also means fixed, settled, stuck.

By those standards, Jay-Z, at 47, might seem old. Standards are presumptuous, though, because, really, what do we know about "old" rappers? Only that they don't rap as much as they used to. I mean, they're still around — but as part of back-patting nostalgia (in concert or on HBO) or hosting the Grammys or cooking with Martha Stewart. Maybe they've still got it. But vital new music is secondary at best.

Despite a lot of lucrative distractions, Jay-Z is still a rapper, whose voice, apparently, still matters. "Apparently," because I didn't expect much from "4:44," his 13th solo (or solo-ish) record that arrived, as heavily advertised, at the end of June.

But it's better than good: a gorgeously produced stab at self-examination (it runs less than the length of a standard therapy session) that suggests a new direction for rap's elder statesmen. It also demonstrates a way that certain black artists can reckon with middle age — by accepting the emotionalism, humor and self-criticism that come naturally to a current generation of younger rappers.

Anybody irritated by the posturing of Jay-Z's previous album, "Magna Carta: Holy Grail" (2013), was likely put off by the prospect of more. If a major rapper arrives at his mid-40s and wants to give us a song that mentions fine wines and a serial-killer drug dealer, then drops the name of a fashion-designer-movie-director more than a dozen times ("Tom Ford"), maybe he should be hosting the Grammys, too.

Jay-Z in 2007.

It's entirely possible that Jay-Z arrived to record "Magna Carta" aware that there's not much of a road map for a rapper in his 40s, especially one whose body of work and reputation are great enough to haunt him. His clever, brash, kaleidoscopically grim 1996 debut, "Reasonable Doubt," is as much a work of memoir of life in the street-level drug trade as it is an album.

On it, he raps with the impunity of a mafia don. It's a distinction that's always kept him seeming a little older than everybody else, while, eventually, holding his competitors' youth against them. On songs like "Change Clothes," with Pharrell, from 2003, and "Off That," with a young-and-hungry Drake, from 2009, he was all too happy to display a cranky old-soul impatience, arguing that because he thinks he is grown up, his peers should, too.

"Y'all [epithet] acting way too tough/Throw on a suit, and get it tapered up," he implored on "Change Clothes."

But eventually that sense of superiority came to sound like an exercise. Rap is a language art, and no matter your age, you need something to say. The problem with "Magna Carta" wasn't that Jay-Z was too old. It is that he sounded bored. The music was disconnected from life, and his materialism sounded passé even for hip-hop. Fashion, art, love, even philanthropy were spiked with a testy self-consciousness. The whole thing reeked of midlife crisis.

"4:44" sounds like a consequence of that crisis. Maybe Jay-Z was bored in his 40s. Maybe he cheated on his wife, Beyoncé. He bought expensive stuff and maybe needed to brag about it. Maybe he was as skeptical and uncertain as we were about what such a person should be rapping about.

Then Beyoncé released "Lemonade," and more or less told him. It arrived in the spring of 2016 and announced to the world that his sense of risk — as a former drug dealer, an entrepreneur and a womanizer — has a cost: her love.

It's believable that Jay-Z really had run out of fresh ideas. But if he were going to keep making new records, "Lemonade" demanded at least a partial response to Beyoncé's agony and the scope of her artistry.

The resulting album isn't trying to match either. "Lemonade" is a fully processed, entirely emotional performance. "4:44" is Tony Soprano at his first couple of sessions with Dr. Melfi. He's not totally sure why he's here and is occasionally petty about it. Jay-Z acknowledges the pain he caused without entirely agreeing to own it.

It's the production, by the longtime hip-hop and R&B producer No I. D., that most gives the album its psychology. He puts samples by the Alan Parsons Project, Stevie Wonder, Nina Simone, the Clark Sisters and Hannah Williams & the Affirmations to masterly use. Where Jay-Z is inclined to be passive, the music insinuates. It makes him seem more culpable, vulnerable, spiritual and transparent than he might even realize. No I. D. is a studio wizard. He's also Dr. Melfi.

Jay-Z's old creative and sexual promiscuity have been replaced by an act of commitment. No more women, just his wife. No more gluts of great producers, just this one. These are the new risks for him: monogamy, focus, trust. There are new existential concerns, too. The ambition here extends from his own plight to the straits of black people all over America. Nothing like a coherent thesis emerges, but he's feeling his way toward if not a moral capitalism then the idea of who capitalism is for.

Jay-Z began his career talking about all the money he had and how he made it. Now, he's aged into a man with time to think about what the money means, what else it can do. He has become wealthy, and wealth is money with dimension, vision and heirs.

Every time I'm reading a magazine and see one of those ads for a Patek Philippe watch, I take a second to wonder about the meaning of wealth. (This is a timepiece you take out a mortgage for.) The ads usually feature two or three generations of handsome white people, and the tag line is something obnoxiously poignant, like "You never actually own a Patek Philippe. You merely look after it for the next generation."

It's a mission statement about legacy and affluence that's rarely mentioned in rap, which is sometimes pathologically obsessed with the optics of spending. Saving never comes up. Neither does nonmusical posterity. To be fair, what's sexy about those?

Promiscuity is a rap subject. Paternity, not so much. Young men, understandably, aren't too concerned with the future. New money tends to burn holes in pockets. Putting something away, having something to hand down, those tend to be old-person concerns. Certainly, other rappers have wills. But Jay-Z is actually ruminating about his. He's wondering, too, whether your money's doing all it can.

On "4:44," he gets churlish about that. In "The Story of O. J.," he asks and answers, "You know what's more important than spending money in a strip club? Credit."

A line later, he is asking, regrettably, if we know why the Jews own all the property in America. His phrasing perpetuates one stereotype to emphasize another about black people and capital — that, compared with white people, they have none. His pointing this out at 47 requires you to know what he was like when he was 27, when the gentleman at the club was him.

Some of the risk of being an old rapper is that the old posturing won't do. You actually have to stand for something. Jay-Z also has to reckon with where he has stood — with the Obamas on one hand but also cavalierly against womankind on the other. What does he make of his track record, his history, say, with women, and what will his children make of that?

Maybe this is why young rappers don't rap old. The evolving nature of maturity can make you seem like a hypocrite.

This idea of legacy becomes a halting socioeconomic lecture on "4:44." He's working hard for his estate so that death won't leave a hole. It will leave a whole. This is an ultrapractical view of the end of life that testifies to the sort of bootstrap conservatism that argues that because one black person has overcome the systemic and self-inflicted roadblocks to success, anyone can. These are his rags-to-riches racial politics. He's made his black life matter, so should you.

The emotional twist on "4:44" is that despite years of his rapping about the empire he's built, he didn't know its value until he almost lost the woman who helped build it. Maybe he was being too much of a man to notice. Not long after the album's release, Jay-Z put out an awkwardly short companion video in which famous black men (and Aziz Ansari) discuss being lovers and fathers and living at an emotional disadvantage in relationships with women. It's fascinating but also probably beside the point of his adultery. The video's point is: We black men can talk about the difficulties of being black men. We can emote!

You saw something like that a couple of weeks ago on an episode of "The Bachelorette" when a suitor — one of the very last — named Eric sincerely warns Rachel that his life in Baltimore isn't as posh as in some of the show's European locations or as stable as those of the white men he is up against. Eric started as a cutup. But we are supposed to believe that Rachel has grown him up. And so his moving admission of mere circumstantial inferiority (he's poor) was meant to enhance his worth as a man.

The beauty of Barry Jenkins's romance "Moonlight" — some of it, anyway — is the way it didn't have to work half as hard to let you see deep inside a character who over time graduates from impressionable child to impenetrable adult thug. You never lose sight of the emotional void that he winds up driving half the night to fill.

As popular culture archetypes, these used to be scary black men. But every once in a while, they're granted a humanity that, with old-school rappers, is harder to come by. It's not an art form that forgives weakness, concession or blame. It runs on burnishing and destroying egos. It thrives on the performance of flawless maximal authenticity and lyrical supremacy. Jay-Z doesn't relinquish his ego on "4:44." But on "Kill Jay-Z," the rueful opening song, he contemplates the downsides of having such a strong one: "Die Jay-Z, this ain't back in the days/You don't need an alibi, Jay-Z/Cry Jay-Z, we know the pain is real/But you can't heal what you never reveal."

This is Jay-Z driving half the night, to some place we've never seen him go, perhaps to some place he's never even been. But part of maturity — whether or not you're a rapper — is being human enough to accept that the first step is getting in the car.

# CHAPTER 2

# Nicki Minaj

Nicki Minaj (born Onika Tanya Maraj) has built her reputation in the rap world with her distinctive and playful
voice and lyrics. Releasing her debut album "Pink Friday"
in 2009, Minaj has received multiple Grammy nominations and topped the Billboard charts. As a woman in
a male-dominated industry, she has incorporated her
sexuality and identity into her music. The articles in this
section show her critical reception and her
cultural significance.

## Nicki Minaj's 'The Pinkprint'

REVIEW | BY JON CARAMANICA | DEC. 15, 2014

PART OF THE MAGIC of the modern record business is that the worth of
the album has been diminished. Almost anything can be a great album
now — a mixtape, a cluster of songs on Soundcloud, a dump of digital
files. That to some the album still has a sort of aesthetic integrity, that
it should mean something different from the rest of their creative output, is an increasingly old-fashioned idea.

Meet Nicki Minaj, fuddy duddy. Ms. Minaj still sees inherent aesthetic worth in the album form and is willing to remold herself to
achieve something in that space that she hasn't elsewhere.

Over the last five years, Ms. Minaj the pop striver has often gotten
in the way of Ms. Minaj the fearsome rapper. But Ms. Minaj is already
a pop idol because of her fearsome rapping (and her outsize personality, though those are related phenomena); the idea that a different
approach is necessary to bolster her fame is antiquated.

"The Pinkprint" is her third studio album, and like the first two it's full of compromises and half-successes. Sometimes she wants to be cousins with OneRepublic, sometimes Lil Wayne. And she succeeds at both, though only one of those goals is noble. Where Ms. Minaj stumbles is that the more earnest her subject matter, the more direct and deliberate her flow. As a rapper, she's capable of grand technical feats, rapid cadence switching and complex rhyme patterns, but generally she puts those fireworks to the side when diving deep into her feelings.

One song that successfully bridges both approaches is "Bed of Lies," which Ms. Minaj purportedly wrote about the dissolution of her longtime relationship with a man who drained her. "Put you in the crib and you ain't never pay a bill in it/I was killin' it, now you got me poppin' pills in it," she raps.

But when Ms. Minaj thins out her gift in service of a catchy pop mean, it smacks false. If a song like "The Night Is Still Young" were released by someone like, say, Pitbull, it might pass muster, simply because no one expects more of him. But on Ms. Minaj, it's a poor fit.

It's no surprise then that the most successful song from this album thus far has been "Anaconda," a craven revision of Sir Mix-A-Lot's "Baby Got Back," a pop-rap staple, enhanced with Ms. Minaj's jokey limerick-esque stories. But it's nowhere near the best. Far better are the songs in which Ms. Minaj lets her rap freak flag fly — "Four Door Aventador," which has echoes of Biggie Smalls, or the rowdy "Trini Dem Girls," or her transcendently bawdy verse on "Only." But when it comes to more traditional songs, Ms. Minaj too often leans on sap, and rarely do the singers who she imports to contribute hooks (when she's not singing them) firmly imprint their personalities. Even Beyoncé is underused on the jumpy "Feeling Myself."

In this way, Ms. Minaj is a Christina Aguilera in need of her Linda Perry, an Elton John in search of a Bernie Taupin — not to write verses, which Ms. Minaj is outlandishly capable of, but to build songs with.

All the raw material is there. By at least one measure, Ms. Minaj has had as ferocious a year as any rapper. Consider her alternate

2014 — a sharp-fanged appearance on Beyoncé's "Flawless" remix; her headspinning rhymes on the unprintably-titled song from the Young Money label compilation that's shortened to "Lookin"; a playful verse on Trey Songz's "Touchin' Lovin' "; and song-stealing remixes of YG's "My Hitta," Young Thug's "Danny Glover," Rae Sremmurd's "No Flex Zone," and more. A few more of these, and you'd have a decent-length set of songs better than most any major label hip-hop album this year, including this one.

# Nicki Minaj: Black Women 'Rarely Rewarded' for Pop Culture Contributions

BY KATIE ROGERS | JULY 22, 2015

THE RAPPER Nicki Minaj reacted on Tuesday to not being nominated for MTV's coveted Video of the Year award by saying that the cultural contributions of black women are often overlooked, raising the specter of racism in the music industry, and setting off a Twitter debate that drew thousands of people — including Taylor Swift.

Ms. Minaj, whose music video for "Anaconda" held a video streaming record until it was broken by Ms. Swift's "Bad Blood" video in May, felt that "Anaconda" and "Feeling Myself," a collaboration with Beyoncé, should have been nominated. (Another video by Beyoncé, "7/11," was.) Ms. Minaj did garner nods for other MTV Video Music Awards.

The jungled-themed "Anaconda" video featured curvy women dancing and gyrating in a series of flesh-baring outfits. The video, which samples heavily from Sir Mix-a-Lot's "Baby Got Back" put women front-and-center rather than behind a male rapper. It was an instant hit online.

The single's cover art, which featured Ms. Minaj crouching in a thong, was also a hit, and turned the image into a commodity. Users created a meme of the cover that featured SpongeBob SquarePants, Marge Simpson and Facebook's logo, among other universally recognized cultural symbols.

In a series of tweets, Ms. Minaj hinted that "Anaconda" would have been nominated if she had been a different type of woman or "kind" of artist. She also said that black women were rarely given appropriate credit for their cultural contributions.

And that is when Taylor Swift got involved.

Nicki Minaj performs onstage during the 2015 BET Awards on June 28, 2015, in Los Angeles, California.

The video for Ms. Swift's "Bad Blood," a collaboration with the rapper Kendrick Lamar, features the actresses Lena Dunham, Mariska Hargitay and Selena Gomez. It also showcases a bevy of white models whose bodies are considered the standard for beauty in the fashion and lingerie industry: Karlie Kloss, Lily Aldridge, Martha Hunt and Gigi Hadid. The video features a lot less twerking and only slightly more clothing than "Anaconda."

Ms. Swift collected nine nominations this year.

The exchange was quickly seen by the media as a feud, and fans of Ms. Minaj got involved to comment on the broader issue of race in music and to critique Ms. Swift's response as being indicative of a brand of feminism dominated by white women.

Other comments earned a quick retweet by Ms. Minaj, including one that called on Ms. Swift to support black women in the industry.

The Video Music Awards will be shown on Aug. 30. In the meantime, the conversation about race and double standards is sure to continue on Twitter.

Miley Cyrus, who took home last year's top honor for her "Wrecking Ball" video, has abstained from the latest debate — except to say that she is hosting this year's show.

Ms. Cyrus's triumphant winning video featured her both nude and in white panties, swinging from the ceiling and licking a sledgehammer.

# Nicki Minaj and Meek Mill, Twitter's Ethics Police

BY JON CARAMANICA | JULY 24, 2015

THIS WAS A WEEK for rumbles, for striking back at unchallenged wisdom. Sometimes the desire to speak truth to power is so strong it outweighs any backlash that such interjections might cause. Sometimes that's exactly the point.

Witness the recent conflagrations initiated by Nicki Minaj and Meek Mill. They have been an item for several months and are currently on tour together — Ms. Minaj is the headliner, of course. On Tuesday, both took to Twitter with fast, feeling-motivated fingers. Ms. Minaj was concerned about how the media normalizes and rewards certain types of beauty above others; Meek Mill was focused on preserving truthfulness in a genre that's long prized it. As the smoke cleared, it became evident that hip-hop's most prominent new couple are also the new ethics police, animated by principle and standing firm and tall.

Ms. Minaj went first. On Tuesday, after not receiving an MTV Video Music Award nomination for video of the year (though she did receive other nods), she underscored what she believed was a persistent bias in the kind of videos that receive attention: "If your video celebrates women with very slim bodies, you will be nominated for vid of the year," she wrote on Twitter. She was aggrieved but cool, reasonably assailing the ways in which the mainstream often diminishes the work of black women. Whether the VMAs were the most appropriate hill to take a stand on is an open question, but they were the available one.

One of the nominated videos was Taylor Swift's model-filled "Bad Blood" — Ms. Minaj didn't mention it directly, but Ms. Swift did the work for her. Shortly after Ms. Minaj's tweet, Ms. Swift, seemingly in a spasm of if-the-tweet-fits pique, replied: "I've done nothing but love & support you. It's unlike you to pit women against each other. Maybe one of the men took your slot."

Cue earthquake. Ms. Swift was quickly given a lesson in intersectional feminism, which highlights the fact that women of different backgrounds experience oppression differently. Ms. Minaj hadn't been pitting woman against woman — she had been highlighting the failures of an ostensibly fair system. By framing Ms. Minaj's critique as an attack only on her own success, it was Ms. Swift who ended up causing friction.

Again, in response, Ms. Minaj was cool, reasonable: "Huh? U must not be reading my tweets. Didn't say a word about u. I love u just as much. But u should speak on this." This was an invitation, not a provocation. (Katy Perry, doubtless thrilled to see Ms. Swift on the defensive, also chimed in to point out that "Bad Blood," which is rumored to be about tensions between the two, is itself a song that pits woman against woman.)

Ms. Swift's gaffe underscores the limitations of public displays of affinity as compared with public (or private, for that matter) challenges to systems that exist to further privilege for those already in possession of it. (Her challenge to Apple Music's pay system was a rare foray into controversy.) Even Ms. Swift's follow-up mea culpa — telling Ms. Minaj: "If I win, please come up with me!! You're invited to any stage I'm ever on" — relies on that same currency (and also on Ms. Swift's victory). Friendship has value, but it is not a panacea.

Later on Tuesday night, Meek Mill decided he didn't have much use for friends anyhow. In a hail of tweets, he accused Drake of relying on a ghostwriter for the verse that he rapped on Meek Mill's latest album, "Dreams Worth More Than Money."

"He ain't even write that verse on my album and if I woulda knew I woulda took it off my album..... I don't trick my fans! Lol," he said on Twitter.

Ghostwriting has a long and semi-secretive history in hip-hop. It's still largely perceived as taboo, even if some of rap's biggest stars rely on collaborators for lyric ideas. In this case, Quentin Miller, the rapper Meek Mill identified as the behind-the-scenes assister, is a credited songwriter on several songs on Drake's recent album, "If You're Reading This It's Too Late." (Seemingly underscoring Meek Mill's point, a vocal reference demo of Mr. Miller rapping a different Drake song was leaked this week.)

By Wednesday night, Meek Mill had apologized to Ms. Minaj onstage at their tour stop in Virginia — she and Drake are friends and labelmates. There they were, two lovers answering to each other and no one else. She petted him eagerly, like a hungry cat.

Unsurprisingly, Ms. Swift and Drake are similar targets. They are widely admired and commercially successful, and also loathed in some corners for what might be termed an excess of sincerity (or at minimum, the performance of such). Each has turned that earnestness, which could be a liability, into an asset. Drake weaves it into his music; you (generally) can't reveal something about him he hasn't already revealed himself. Ms. Swift never appears anything less than enthused and gracious in public.

For both of them, friendship — or the appearance of it — is essential to the expansion of their empires. Ms. Swift has lately publicly embraced supermodels (Karlie Kloss, Lily Aldridge), other singers (Selena Gomez, Lorde), actresses (Hailee Steinfeld, Sarah Hyland) and even Kendrick Lamar. A cynical read is that these connections have been a way to shift conversation away from her relationships, which for a few years drowned out most other public discourse around her. Alternately, it's not inconceivable to believe that all those people (and millions more) would jump at the chance to be Ms. Swift's friend.

Ms. Swift's alliances are social and Instagram friendly; Drake's, though, are professional and sonic. Several times in the past few years, he's identified impressive young artists early, and found a way to collaborate, either by bringing them into the studio (as he did with the Weeknd, for his 2011 album "Take Care") or by offering his services for a remix, as he's done with Future, iLoveMakonnen, Migos, Fetty Wap and others.

If Drake and Ms. Swift excel at currying favor and finding common ground, Ms. Minaj and Meek Mill have walked bolder, at times lonelier paths. Collecting friends far and wide is not their goal. Ms Minaj has long pointed out what she perceives as mistreatment or hypocrisy in the music business. Meek Mill, one of the last remaining mainstream rappers still loyal to the street rap of the 1990s, has barely tweaked his approach in search of wider acclaim.

Those principles serve as nourishment, and also as weapons — compromise is the enemy. Drake hasn't replied directly to Meek Mill's accusations. But in a private message made public on Instagram, he wrote: "I signed up for greatness. This comes with it." And he has liked an Instagram video that places a magazine cover featuring Skepta (a Drake buddy) in front of one featuring Meek Mill.

As for Ms. Swift, on Thursday she took to Twitter to apologize for her misstep: "I thought I was being called out. I missed the point, I misunderstood, then misspoke. I'm sorry, Nicki." Maybe Ms. Swift will get her friend back, or maybe she'll get schooled on what friendship could really mean.

# Nicki Minaj Raps Life Lessons at Barclays Center

REVIEW | BY JON CARAMANICA | JULY 27, 2015

"PROMISE ME that you'll never let anyone steal your joy": Sunday night at Barclays Center in Brooklyn, Nicki Minaj was convening her faithful, guiding them through whatever storms they'd been weathering.

From the beginning of her two-hour-plus set, she'd been weaving aphorisms and pep talks between songs. She was sure to remind the crowd of the significance of the moment, that all of them — herself included — were in "an arena being headlined by a little girl from Queens that raps."

But perhaps Ms. Minaj's greatest accomplishment is that it's become easy to take her success as a given. She is an artist without precedent — a female rapper who's an astounding technician, a style original and a pop superstar. And also one of her musical generation's greatest advocates for self-reliance and grass-roots feminism, as seen in action last week during the tweet storm that began as a lesson in media acknowledgment and representations of black women and ended with an apology from Taylor Swift, pop's leading light.

That blowup, though, threatened to become a distraction from the fact that Ms. Minaj is at the helm of the best hip-hop tour lineup of the year. In addition to Meek Mill, the rapper who is also Ms. Minaj's boyfriend — this tour has become a working vacation for the couple, it seems — the bill also included the caffeinated Southern-brother duo Rae Sremmurd, the Janet Jackson disciple Tinashe and the modestly sly young female rapper Dej Loaf.

In total, the lineup reflected Ms. Minaj's many parts — tough, sultry, exuberant, colorful, exaggerated. In her own herky-jerky set, though, she was toggling among approaches: street-wise songs, saccharine pop hits, collaborations, collisions of all these. Ms. Minaj's catalog is so varied, she has colonized so much turf in so many spaces, that unifying it under one umbrella is a challenge.

What remained the same throughout the night was her verve. It was there in her life-coach lessons, it was there in her sassy but casual dancing (leaving the harder steps to her backup troupe), and it was there in her vocal approach. Ms. Minaj has a way of vocally heaving her most poignant lines — it's part chest-puffery, part comic exaggeration. Often she's rapping through a grin, striking a pose for the camera, but when she lets the facade down and focuses on the shape and pace of her words, she's a bulldozer.

Ms. Minaj is such a dense rapper that the specifics can become lost in a show of this size. Other great technical rappers have dealt with this problem in different ways: Eminem began to gear his music toward the anthemic, filling arenas with big, brooding rock choruses; Jay Z, on the other hand, uses silence and stopping and starting for emphasis. Ms. Minaj has a simpler solution: Relying on her rabid fans, who rapped along so intensely to even her more obscure songs that she didn't have to bother.

Near the end of the night, Ms. Minaj surprised the crowd with an appearance by Lil Wayne, the head of her label, Young Money, who has been embroiled in a sticky, possibly violent standoff with Baby, his longtime mentor. Just 32, Lil Wayne is a beleaguered elder at this point, and Ms. Minaj's embrace of him was pointed — they called each other the greatest rapper alive, they held hands, they hugged.

Given the week Ms. Minaj and her boyfriend have had, a reminder of happier times was in order. Drake is also signed to Young Money, and the rift last week between him and Meek Mill most likely tested alliances and friendships. During his set, Meek Mill continued the attacks on Drake he started last week, accusing him of not writing the verse he contributed to Meek Mill's album.

One of Drake's most refined skills has been collaboration — nearly everyone of note in hip-hop over the past few years, large or small, has relied on his services at one point or another. Ms. Minaj and Meek Mill performed songs that they collaborated on with Drake — "Amen" for Meek Mill; for Ms. Minaj, among others, "Make Me Proud" and "Up All Night" (on that one she did emphasize Drake's line, "I don't really know who I'ma lose this year," which was maybe a taunt).

Those were passing concerns — this was a night about the happy couple. Meek Mill sped through several of his blustery hits — a minute of one, then another, like a one-sided mixed-martial-arts bout. He's a shouter, and an arena suits him well, even if his muscular rap is all but out of vogue these days. But part of his recent evolution has been a willingness to show his softer side. His set included a deeply moving segment in which he rapped at a photo of his father, who died when he was a boy, displayed on a huge screen behind him.

And as has become their wont on this tour, the couple shared the stage at the end of the night, performing their tepid collaborations from Meek Mill's new album, songs that do neither any favors. That didn't matter, though. They made eyes at each other. She kissed him, then playfully pushed him away. He called her "the girl that got me star-struck," echoing an insult Drake sent in his direction on a song last week. Candid and not-so-candid photos of the two of them cycled on a screen.

This is hip-hop love in 2015 — public, provocative, not altogether unstrategic. "Anything you can think in your mind you can physically do," Ms. Minaj had told the crowd earlier. "Everybody that doesn't have your best interests at heart just falls away."

# The Passion of Nicki Minaj

BY VANESSA GRIGORIADIS | OCT. 7, 2015

POP MUSIC is dominated almost exclusively by the female star —
Beyoncé, Rihanna, Katy Perry, Taylor Swift, Miley Cyrus, Lady Gaga
and, as always, Madonna. Engaging in a frantic, complex game — crossing over many genres to keep up with the current caldron of hip-hop,
electronic music and R&B; signing sponsorship deals to make up for
the lack of album sales; performing live everywhere from sheikhs' parties to worldwide arenas — these women are the pop business now, and
they're not feeling particularly shy about telling us that. Their primary
message has become one of being the woman you actually have to be
behind the scenes to succeed today: powerful, outspoken and in control.

Nicki Minaj is the world's biggest female hip-hop star, a top pop star
and the first woman to achieve success in both genres. Like Beyoncé,
who performed recently in Central Park with the words "boss" and
"hustler" flashing on screens behind her, along with a grainy video
in which she smashed a vacuum and a sewing machine, Minaj has
become expert at modeling the ways that women can wield power in
the industry. But she has also drawn attention to the ways in which
power can be embodied by a woman standing up for herself and speaking her own mind. Minaj's behavior isn't exclusive to her tracks; she
also exhibits it in the national telenovela that she, like the rest of these
women, to a greater or lesser degree, is running about herself, feeding
the public information about her paramours, ex-paramours, peccadil-
loes and beefs, all of it delivered in social media's short, sharp bursts.

Perhaps you recall the three-act revenge drama that played out on
various screens last month, as Minaj faced off against two major pow-
ers: Swift, the 25-year-old golden girl who may be the richest woman
in music, and who spends time wholesomely baking cookies at her
TriBeCa spread with a rotating cast of B.F.F.s; and Cyrus, the ex-
Disney star who, more than five years ago, was extolling the virtues

of purity rings but is now America's pre-eminent "bad girl." She first recreated herself as a pornified star who wore gold grilles on her teeth and introduced the mainstream to "twerking," a dance originating in black circles in the South that involves shaking your buttocks, and more recently rebranded herself a "happy hippie" and "genderqueer," neither male nor female.

Pop stars today travel around with a small entourage, conducting their business from a mobile phone in the back of a climate-controlled luxury vehicle. And you can imagine these women in their cars when the nominations for MTV's Video Music Awards, which long ago stopped judging musical quality and moved on to assessing the size of empires, were announced earlier this summer. The list did not include a nod in the top award category for Minaj's wild video for "Anaconda," a song that samples Sir Mix-a-Lot's "Baby Got Back," from 1992. The video features Minaj flipping the script to be the baby who has back, refusing to let her co-star, Drake, touch her buttocks and, somewhat frighteningly (for men) cutting up a banana that's a clear metaphor for the snake in their pants.

You can picture Minaj in her Maybach as she considered this particular affront and then used it to make a larger point. "If I was a different 'kind' of artist, 'Anaconda' would be nominated," she tweeted, followed by "If your video celebrates women with very slim bodies, you will be nominated," and "I'm not always confident. Just tired. Black women influence pop culture so much but are rarely rewarded for it." (For the record, Beyoncé was nominated for the award in question, for a video in which she dances around in underwear and, inexplicably, a sweatshirt with the word "KALE.")

Swift, the good girl, herself nominated for a video featuring semi-clad, slender women, jumped in next: "I've done nothing but love & support you. It's unlike you to pit women against each other. Maybe one of the men took your slot." (She quickly encountered media pushback and called Minaj to apologize.) But the free spirit Cyrus had something to say, too: A few weeks later, in this newspaper, she criticized Minaj's comments as lacking an "open heart" and "love," adding that she didn't respect Minaj's statement "because of the anger that came with it," calling it "not very polite" and continuing, "Nicki Minaj is not too kind."

Soon, our characters gathered in the V.M.A. Thunderdome, where things that are not quite true are staged in a crude, middle-school-esque pageant, with players jockeying for time. And indeed, Swift and Minaj, having reached a truce, opened the show together. But later, as Minaj slinked onstage in a revealing dress that closely resembled gold filigree on a china cup to accept her award — for Best Hip-Hop Video, which is not as important as Video of the Year: "I saw [Cyrus] just looking at me, with her face screwed up, and I thought, What the!" she told me in mid-September, in the Trump hotel in Columbus Circle, while visiting New York for Fashion Week. Onstage, Minaj next did something exceedingly rare in the commercial music world. She addressed Cyrus with real venom — "This bitch that had a lot to say about me the other day in the press" — and pointed at her with a manicured finger: "Miley, what's good?" MTV cut Minaj's mike, but you could see her lips forming the words, "Don't play with me, bitch."

A month later, the episode was still bothering Minaj. Addressing Cyrus, she told me: "The fact that you feel upset about me speaking on something that affects black women makes me feel like you have some big balls. You're in videos with black men, and you're bringing out black women on your stages, but you don't want to know how black women feel about something that's so important? Come on, you can't want the good without the bad. If you want to enjoy our culture and our lifestyle, bond with us, dance with us, have fun with us, twerk with us, rap with us, then you should also want to know what affects us, what is bothering us, what we feel is unfair to us. You shouldn't not want to know that."

**Minaj stands a** bit over five feet tall, and as she padded around barefoot in her hotel suite, there was a tangle of shoes and outfits collected nearby that she had considered but rejected for Fashion Week. Outfits carefully sewn to the measurements of a six-foot-tall model with hipbones like handlebars don't fit a shapely-all-over woman, and

Nicki Minaj accepts the Best Hip-Hop Video award for "Anaconda" onstage during the 2015 MTV Video Music Awards at Microsoft Theater on Aug. 30, 2015, in Los Angeles, Calif.

Minaj, like Kim Kardashian, favors garments with spandex in them. In the last 24 hours, she had poured herself into a nude mesh Alexander Wang dress that the most party-hearty 19-year-old would choose only as a beach cover-up; changed to a fire-engine-red two-piece zip-up suit for Wang's after-party; danced at Jay-Z's 40/40 Club in the Flatiron district for hours; hit the recording studio with her boyfriend, the Philadelphia rapper Meek Mill; then, finally, crawled into bed in the hotel on the Upper West Side at 7 a.m. She woke up at 3:30 p.m., changing into purple leggings and an oversize black T-shirt, though remnants of the night's ensembles remained — her hair swept up in a gun moll's bouffant, a smidge shorter than Amy Winehouse wore hers; several diamond stud earrings crawled up her right ear like a series of buttons on the back of a Victorian gown.

Minaj may have had a fair amount of influence over the fact that pop stars are constantly telling us they're bosses, or they're bitches, or they're "boss bitches," which seems like a contradiction, or redundant, but is said without a trace of irony. A unique figure who draws 10-year-old girls as fans with her Technicolor wigs, sophisticated mimicry and playful attitude, Minaj also assumes a persona as aggressive, dis-happy and vulgar as any man in hip-hop. She electrifies tracks merely by appearing on them, from Kanye West's "Monster" in 2010 ("First things first, I'll eat your brains," she explains) to the electronic dance music artist David Guetta's "Hey Mama," with a video featuring her gyrating in a desert scene resembling Burning Man. She's also the first woman to rise to the very top of the rap game not only as a star but also as a business entity. "My wrists look like I am a jewel thief/But that's just cuz I am a boss bitch/Now macaroni cheese and grill my swordfish," she says in a song entitled, appropriately enough, "Boss Ass Bitch."

There's nothing new about female artists struggling with issues of power and control, but we're far today from the 1990s, when Queen Latifah proclaimed "every time I hear a brother call a girl a bitch or a ho/ Trying to make a sister feel low/You know all that gots to go." "Bitch," in music, used to be an insult, a sneer, and it still can be. But female empowerment is a trend, and the word has been reclaimed — by Minaj, in many a track; by Rihanna, in "Bitch Better Have My Money"; and triumphantly by Madonna, in her recent track "Bitch, I'm Madonna." This is good for business and either good for women or not good for women at all.

In another era, Minaj's sexuality, expressed semi-parodically — pretending she's a Barbie doll; glorifying women dressed as prostitutes and set in red-light-district windows — might have given feminists pause. But in the 2010s, we have entered a different world in pop culture, one in which sexual repression is perceived as burdensome and perhaps even an inability to holistically integrate the body and self. Young people are identifying and exploring formerly unknown, or at least unlabeled, frontiers of sexuality and gender. And the fact that Minaj is in charge of her own objectification (describing her vagina with more words than I thought existed, and then amplifying its power by rhyming those words), as well as her own monetization (overt product placement in videos is a hallmark) has led most feminist voices to applaud her. But the writer Bell Hooks remains unimpressed, saying of "Anaconda" at a New School panel titled "Whose Booty Is This?": "This [expletive] is boring. What does it mean? Is there something that I'm missing that's happening here?"

"The frequency that Nicki works on is not the easiest frequency for us to wrestle with, because it's about autonomy, and who has it, and whether we can actually tell the difference between self-objectification and self-gratification," says Treva B. Lindsey, an assistant professor of women's, gender and sexuality studies at the Ohio State University, continuing: "Do we even know what an autonomous female looks like in pop culture? What does control even mean in such a corporatized mass-media space?"

On hip-hop radio shows, the dominant journalistic genre for the art form, Minaj speaks with a Queens accent, sometimes injecting it with Caribbean flair. But there was no evidence of that at the hotel, where she spoke in a night-after whisper that sounded like the hiss of a record before a song begins to play. "I never was political or preachy, but I'd stop my show and do two minutes of talking to my girls, boosting them up," Minaj said, sitting in a small, straight-backed chair upholstered in the light gray fabric ubiquitous in luxury hotels, Columbus Circle's billboards pulsing in the background as dusk fell. "They'd go home feeling, 'Can't nobody tell me [expletive].'" And as her career went on, she realized she had more to say. "We got so many girls right now having children and don't even know the first thing to say to a child, but you're having a child because 'I want to keep this dude,' or it just happened," she explains on her second album. "Why are we never in control? Why are we stuck with a baby? Why are we always stuck on the welfare line? Why are we always stuck having to beg, borrow and steal to provide for our children? Why do we think it's something wrong for waiting to have a baby, waiting until you're 35 or 36 to have children? Technology has changed — you can wait! Have something to offer them."

Minaj has a shockingly beautiful and complex face, with a wide, high forehead, dark, almond-shaped eyes and deep dimples on both sides of her cheeks that materialize when she smiles. But when asked if she felt confident in her looks as a kid, she said, "Hell, no!" She paused. "Now, I want to take steps to become more aware of who I am, what I like or dislike about my body — why is that?" she said. She mentioned how insecure she felt on Instagram, "where everyone is freaking drop-dead gorgeous." Don't get her wrong, she said: Like most celebrities, she approves the pictures that appear on her Instagram and other social-media accounts. "I get that people put filters on their pictures — I definitely use filters — but I didn't know people retouched," she says, excitedly talking about being in a nightclub the other day, taking pictures with a friend, and how the friend "cleaned all the sweat off our face" before she posted the photo. "We're in a club! We can have a moist, dewy-looking face."

She laughs for the first time in our conversation, dimples popping everywhere, sun radiating through the room. "People" — famous people, she means — "are posting pictures of working out, and then there's a change in their body" most likely from plastic surgery, "and they say it's because they were working out! Ah-hahahaha." Then she turns serious again. "Back in the day, in hip-hop, the thick girl was glorified. Now the rappers are dating skinny white women. So it's almost like, 'Wait a minute, who's going to tell the thick black girls that they're sexy and fly, too?'"

**One of Minaj's** most fascinating stylistic tricks as a performer has been incorporating alter egos, not only the Barbie doll (which she calls Harajuku Barbie) but Roman, an outspoken gay boy who lives inside of her. These alter egos, which have extensively detailed identities, seem exemplary of the way that women are forced to assume different personae to get through the day. But when I asked why she hadn't called on them much on her last album, she gave me a vague answer about how they were only "funny" and were still around somewhere. Early in her career, she also adopted Lady Gaga's method of saturating the media with outrageous costumes, but now, when I asked if Gaga influenced her, she shot back, with a look of such intense disapproval my hair curled: "I don't even want to discuss that. That's so old to me."

Minaj, tough in general, is known to be particularly tough with the press, like rappers tend to be. "You have to be like a beast — that's the only way they respect you," she said, in a soft-focus MTV documentary on her life, explaining that she walks out of photo shoots when there's "a $50 clothes budget and some sliced pickles." She's also guarded about her past, and much of her present. Born Onika Maraj in Trinidad in 1982, she moved to the United States several years later (her parents spent two years in the States before she arrived, trying to get settled). Minaj has long emphasized her difficult upbringing — speaking openly about crack cocaine use in her home, in Jamaica, Queens, as well as domestic abuse and an episode when she says her father tried to burn down her house. But it's difficult to reconcile those stories with the recent announcement that she's developing a show about her youth for ABC Family. When I asked if her father abused her, she said: "No. He was just abusive." She continued: "I would always hear him yelling and cursing, always. And it made me feel it was the way to interact, because that's how I saw him interacting." She said her parents' marriage wasn't a happy one. "When I was younger," she explained, "I thought that the only reason my mother didn't leave my father was for financial reasons." She went on: "From early on in my life, I looked at a woman not having her money as the biggest curse," and then added, "Now that I'm an adult, I realize that women stay whether a man's rich or poor. It's just a weakness."

Like Lady Gaga, who starred in plays while attending the Upper East Side's Convent of the Sacred Heart, Minaj has drama-school chops. She studied theater at the Upper West Side's LaGuardia High School — the school from "Fame" — working on her freestyle rap skills in the lunchroom. After graduation, she waitressed at Red Lobster to make money and sang choruses on low-level rappers' tracks. One day in a recording studio, she asked a local artist if she could write a rap. "I wrote eight bars while he was in the booth, and he asked to hear it, but I was too shy. I said, 'Can I just go spit it?' " Minaj was in her neighborhood when she heard the song booming out of his car. "He was playing it proudly, and that was my first indication — maybe I'm good." She began locking herself in her room for hours and hours with her beat CDs, she says. "Eventually my mother would come in to check if I was alive."

Minaj's darkest period may have started when she tried to make it in the men's world of hip-hop, in about 2002. But when I asked for details, she said, "I'm not approving or confirming anything you said." A sketch for this time, then, begins when producers placed her in a group called the Hoodstars with three men, including Safaree Samuels, who would become her boyfriend of a decade; failing to secure a recording contract, Minaj began to rebuild herself as a solo act. In 2006, another producer, Big Fendi, christened her Nicki Minaj ("Fendi flipped [my name] when he met me because I had such a nasty flow! I eat bitches!" she said, in an early interview). He reimagined her as the new Lil' Kim. Kim, the Biggie Smalls protégée, wore wigs, pretended to be a black Barbie and not only rapped about her genitalia but called attention to it in photo shoots that Minaj recreated. (At some point, Minaj also sold her mixtapes out of her white BMW 323i, a car she says she scrimped and saved to buy. I'm not sure when that was, because after I asked about it twice, she told me it was a dumb question.)

Enticing big-name rappers to add a couple of bars to your tracks, or securing a guest spot on one of those rappers' songs, is the way to build fame in hip-hop, and Minaj proved herself to be adept. She garnered guest verses from hip-hop royalty, including Lil Wayne. But her manager at the time, Debra Antney, who was born in Jamaica, Queens, before becoming an Atlanta hip-hop matriarch (and also the rapper Waka Flocka Flame's mother), says, "Nicki was the timidest little girl you'd ever want to see in your life — she was so broken up, but she was so determined, all in one breath." Timid? "I used to have to scream at her: 'You're not going to sit here and cry, you're not going to let nobody shut you down, that's what you're not going to do,' " she says.

Nicki Minaj and rapper Lil Wayne perform onstage during the 2013 Billboard Music Awards at the MGM Grand Garden Arena on May 19, 2013, in Las Vegas, Nev.

Minaj knew with whom she preferred to be aligned, though he didn't sign her until 2009: Lil Wayne, whose label, Young Money, is part of Cash Money, co-founded by Bryan Williams, known as Birdman. Wayne is "a master of psychology. This guy has studied words. This guy is a poet," she told Dazed magazine. She was marketed as a multigenre artist from the beginning, writing her own raps but also using the assembly-line process of pop. "Nicki, with her theater background and ability to take on a range of accents, is extremely well suited to the way that pop music is made today, when the artist is a vocal actor not asked to say something that's profound but rather play a role in a song that someone else has written," says John Seabrook, author of "The Song Machine: Inside the Hit Factory." But building her as a brand, long a part of the culture of hip-hop, was "the furthest thing from breezy," says her manager, the Maverick management group co-founder Gee Roberson. Securing a fragrance deal, a Glu mobile game, an alcoholic drink — all of that requires entering executive suites "dominated by men."

During her rise, Minaj didn't publicly announce that she had a boyfriend — she introduced Samuels to the world only as a valued producer, continuing the long tradition of sex symbols appearing sexually available to their fans. She has since changed her attitude about that, and has not been shy about being in love with her current boyfriend, Meek Mill, pointing toward the bedroom whenever his name came up tonight. He recently had his own beef, with Drake, Minaj's labelmate, during which — this is an abridged version — Meek attacked Drake for using a ghostwriter, and Drake struck back with what seemed like an endless series of dis tracks, one of which asks, "Is that a world tour or your girl's tour?" That Minaj managed to stay above this is significant. "Historically in hip-hop, female rappers have always had to stand next to a male rapper in order to maintain relevance, or keep their spark," says Charlamagne Tha God, the outspoken host of the radio station Power 105.1's program "The Breakfast Club." "What happened with Drake and Meek won't have any effect on Nicki at all, and in fact I think Nicki is so strong that she's one of the reasons people haven't completely said Meek is done."

Minaj talked a bit about dealing with men and work. "Since I was 15, I came out of one relationship and went into another relationship," she told me. "In my relationships, I've been told, 'You don't have to work that much.' But I can't stop working, because it's bigger than work to me. It's having a purpose outside any man."

**Meek's beef with** Drake was different from Minaj's beefs with the pop queens. It was an old fight, about authenticity — the oldest dust-up there is in hip-hop. Minaj is fighting newer battles. While discussing the state of women in the music business, I asked about the ethics of "Straight Outta Compton," the N.W.A. biopic that does not include a reference to Dr. Dre's history of abusing women. "I don't know anything about that," she said. Then I asked about the dramatic goings-on at her label: Wayne is suing Birdman for $51 million for withholding fees, and Wayne's tour bus was riddled with bullets in Georgia earlier this year. A federal indictment claims that individuals connected to another Cash Money rapper, Young Thug, may be responsible.

This was not the game Minaj was here to play — interviews in the social-media era are about being adored, not interrogated. It was getting dark outside when I asked about Drake, Meek, Wayne and Williams. Minaj hadn't turned on lights, so she was in shadow. "They're men, grown-ass men," she said. "It's between them." How does it make you feel, I ask? "I hate it," she said. "It doesn't make me feel good. You don't ever want to choose sides between people you love. It's ridiculous. I just want it to be over."

"Is there a part of you that thrives on drama, or is it no, just pain and unpleasantness—"

The room went quiet, but only for an instant.

"That's disrespectful," Minaj said, drawing herself up in the chair. "Why would a grown-ass woman thrive off drama?"

As soon as I said the words, I wished I could dissolve them on my tongue. In pop-culture idiom, "drama" is the province of Real Housewives with nothing better to do than stick their noses where they don't belong. I was more interested in a different kind of drama — the kind worthy of an HBO series, in which your labelmate is releasing endless dis tracks against your boyfriend and your mentor is suing your label president for a king's ransom. But the phrase I used was offensive, and even as I tried to apologize, I only made matters worse.

"What do the four men you just named have to do with me thriving off drama?" she asked. "Why would you even say that? That's so peculiar. Four grown-ass men are having issues between themselves, and you're asking me do I thrive off drama?"

She pointed my way, her extended arm all I could see other than the diamonds glinting in her ears. This wasn't over yet. "That's the typical thing that women do. What did you putting me down right there do for you?" she asked. "Women blame women for things that have nothing to do with them. I really want to know why — as a matter of fact, I don't. Can we move on, do you have anything else to ask?" she continued. "To put down a woman for something that men do, as if they're children and I'm responsible, has nothing to do with you asking stupid questions, because you know that's not just a stupid question. That's a premeditated thing you just did." She called me "rude" and "a troublemaker," said "Do not speak to me like I'm stupid or beneath you in any way" and, at last, declared, "I don't care to speak to you anymore."

I found myself back in the lobby, with its Trumpian brass fixtures and huge chandeliers, with the black bikes stamped "Trump Hotel" tied up in front, and the men in their blue suits coming down the steps jingling change in their pockets, and the regular Upper West Side scene — bankers walking their dogs, tourists on Citibikes going the wrong way, the sound of an express train coming up through the subway grates. Minaj's actions made sense, in some ways: Even though I had no intention of putting her down as a small-minded or silly woman, she was right to call me out. She had the mike and used it to her advantage, hitting the notes that we want stars like her to address right now, particularly those of misogyny and standing up for yourself, even if it involves standing up for yourself against another woman. I didn't know how much of it Minaj really felt, and how much it was a convenient way of maintaining control. I only knew that, in that moment, she was a boss bitch.

**VANESSA GRIGORIADIS** is a contributing writer for The New York Times Magazine. She has profiled many pop stars, including Katy Perry, Taylor Swift and Madonna. This is her first article for the magazine.

# Nicki Minaj Concert in Angola Draws Human Rights Complaint

BY KATIE ROGERS | DEC. 16, 2015

THE HUMAN RIGHTS FOUNDATION is asking Nicki Minaj to reconsider her scheduled performance in Angola on Saturday, citing a list of abuses committed by the president of the oil-rich African nation.

In an Instagram post, the 33-year-old rapper said that she would be performing at a public Christmas festival hosted by the communications company Unitel. In a letter published on Tuesday, the Human Rights Foundation said that the company is controlled, in part, by the daughter of José Eduardo dos Santos, who has ruled the country since 1979.

"Nicki Minaj is a global artist," the group's president Thor Halvorssen, said in a statement. "Millions of people look up to her for creative inspiration. There is no good reason for her to do business with the corrupt Angolan dictatorship and endorse the ruler's family company."

It is not unusual for celebrities to receive seven figures for performing in countries with questionable human rights records. Lately, the celebrities have also been receiving some scrutiny: In 2013, Jennifer Lopez was criticized for accepting $10 million to perform for Gurbanguly Berdymukhammedov, the president of Turkmenistan, who has long been accused of rigging elections and running a repressive government.

Ms. Minaj is likely to be paid well for her visit to the country. In 2013, Mariah Carey received $1 million for traveling to perform in Angola. The two performers have the same manager, the organization said in the letter.

In a profile of Angola published by The New Yorker in June, the writer Michael Specter described rampant inequality in the country — the capital, Luanda, is the most expensive in the world for expatriates to live, yet the country remains one of the world's least-developed nations. (Angola is ranked first in the world for deaths among children under the age of 5.)

Mr. Specter also chronicled the corruption that touches the daily lives of visitors — the traffic police whose bribes must be paid, the extra fees just to be seated at a restaurant and served a bottle of water.

The Humans Rights Foundation said that circumstances are even worse for Angolans. The organization cited the story of Luaty Beirao, a young Angolan rapper who was among 17 people who were jailed in June for discussing a book that covered the topic of nonviolent resistance.

Mr. Beirao had long been an outspoken critic of the government.

"The bottom line is this: if you try to voice your opinions and they happen to be contrary to the government's, you're more than likely to be chased, get a beat down in public places, have your grandmother receive death threats and all sorts of equally nasty deprivations of your basic human rights," Mr. Beirao, 34, told the website OkayAfrica in 2012.

The letter asked Ms. Minaj to consider her reputation for creativity and supporting young people before she heads to Angola.

"What kind of inspirational message is she sending to millions of young Angolans by performing for the dictatorship that has literally stolen their freedom and their future?" it asked.

Ms. Minaj has not directly addressed the criticism in public. On Wednesday, she seemed mostly preoccupied with responding to critics about her album performance, but it appears that the show in Angola is still on — she found time to post again about her show on Twitter. She then followed up that tweet with another: "Every tongue that rises up against me in judgment shall be condemned."

# Nicki Minaj, Always in Control

**BY ROXANE GAY | OCT. 16, 2017**

THE DAY I WAIT in the hotel lobby of the Ritz-Carlton in Battery Park City to meet Nicki Minaj is the start of New York Fashion Week. I am early, and I watch as stylists push an overfull rack of designer clothes out of the elevator. I later learn they are from Alexander Wang, and are dressing Minaj for the designer's show.

In the hall entrance of her suite, there is another rack bulging with outfits. Deeper into the suite, a lean and lanky hairdresser is combing a very long platinum-blond wig. He is wearing a fascinating outfit that includes black leather pants, a description that is doing those pants a great disservice because they are fabulous. He brushes the wig so carefully, so lovingly, that for a moment, I want to be that wig. A few feet away from his gentle ministrations, a makeup artist is organizing makeup and various brushes and other tools of the trade. Everyone speaks in hushed murmurs.

When Minaj enters, from an adjacent chamber, she is a petite wonder, wearing a fluffy white bathrobe, her face naked. After we greet each other with a light handshake, she asks if I mind if she gets her eyes lined. She isn't really asking, nor do I object. She sits in the makeup chair, and the artist begins applying Minaj's trademark black eyeliner with its exaggerated cat's eye flair.

I am stunned by the number of people Minaj has at her service. I also meet her day-to-day manager and personal assistant — who are two different people — and her stylist. In the hall just outside the suite wait a tailor and a couple of other people eager for Minaj's time. She is the center of gravity for a great many professionals, and she wears that responsibility well.

When her eyes are done, Minaj sits on the adjacent couch, arranging her robe to her liking. There is regality in how she sits. That she is wearing a bathrobe is utterly inconsequential. A queen is a queen regardless. A stylist begins presenting her with options for the two events she will attend later that evening — a dinner party and a book launch. She is shown a clingy, see-through dress with a long train, a gorgeously patterned black-and-white leather Balmain gown and a couple of other options. I marvel at the sublime luxury of basically having a human closet.

Finally, Minaj turns to me, offering her full attention, and says, "You want us to start?" as if, this whole time, we've been waiting on me. I want to applaud with appreciation. Yasssss, queen, as they say.

THROUGHOUT HER CAREER, Minaj has demonstrated a discipline and intelligence that is rare among other pop stars of her generation. She has what she describes to me as "the X-factor, which is just the thing you can't put into words." Onika Tanya Maraj was born in Saint James, Trinidad and Tobago, in 1982, and immigrated to Queens, N.Y., with her family at the age of 5. She began her music career singing with various rappers and working odd jobs. When she waitressed, she wrote lyrics constantly on the notepad she used to take orders. There is genuine pleasure in her voice as she reminisces about this. "I would take people's order and then a rap might come to me just by what they're wearing or what they said or did, and I would go in the kitchen and write it down, put it in the back of my little thing or my apron, and by the time I was done I would have all of these sheets of paper thrown around everywhere with raps."

Since then, her career has been a checklist of milestones. In 2009, she was the first woman artist signed to Young Money, the label founded by Lil Wayne. Three mixtapes and three studio albums — "Pink Friday" in 2010, "Pink Friday: Roman Reloaded" in 2012 and "The Pink Print" in 2014 — followed, and in March 2017, Minaj surpassed Aretha Franklin for the most appearances (76) by a woman on the Billboard Hot 100, a record Franklin had held for almost 40 years. She is the rare hip-hop artist who has successfully and sustainably crossed over into pop music. Minaj, M.I.A. and Madonna performed their single,

"Give Me All Your Luvin," at the 2012 Super Bowl. Days later she performed solo at the Grammy Awards. Her dance song "Starships" went platinum six times over. She even collaborated with Ariana Grande on 2016's song "Side to Side," and while the pairing was unexpected given Grande's previously wholesome image, the song went triple platinum. Minaj does not temper her swagger or sexuality. Sometimes, when I am daydreaming, I marvel at the phrases "dick bicycle" and "If you wanna ménage I got a tricycle" from "Side to Side," which are so damn clever and funny and vulgar but also accurate as hell for a song Grande once described as being "about riding leading to soreness."

Minaj's music is characterized by urgent lyrics, spitting in a range of voices and accents. Her rhymes range from bold and aggressive, to coquettish, to wanton and sultry, with a soupçon of women's empowerment. The pace of her rapping is often breathless but her diction is impeccable. There is wit and sly humor in her work. Take the 2014 single "Only" where Minaj raps, "My man full, he just ate, I don't duck nobody but tape/ Yeah, that was a setup for a punch line on duct tape." She quite simply broadened the definition of hip-hop, making it more joyful, energetic and robust.

Nicki Minaj is also coming down with a cold. Yes, I know what I did there, but it also happens to be true. When we meet, she has just missed a rehearsal for an upcoming performance at Philipp Plein's runway show because of the encroaching sickness, and is medicating herself with Theraflu, NyQuil and rest. Having to fly to New York did not help. Minaj was in Miami (where she now spends most of her time) working on her fourth studio album, the title of which is, for now, a well-kept secret but is "super, super iconic."

That studio time begot the beginnings of her cold — the air-conditioning always blasting, shutting off, blasting again — a vicious cycle of climate control. Minaj ended up spending two nights in the studio because it was one of those sessions where she was able to "write and record and listen back and have excitement in all three of those stages."

It took a long time to get to that place, Minaj tells me, and now, "sonically, I know what the album's about to sound like. I know what this album is gonna mean to my fans. This album is everything in my life coming full circle and me being truly, genuinely happy. It feels almost like a celebration. The last album, 'The Pink Print,' was almost like my diary, closing the chapter on certain things and not knowing if I was happy or sad about beginning new chapters. I was really writing about feeling unsure. Now, I can tell you guys what happened for the last two years of my life. I know who I am. I am getting Nicki Minaj figured out with this album and I'm loving her."

MINAJ'S PUBLIC IMAGE and personas are carefully curated. The tabloids have assiduously tracked her professional and personal lives and I restrain myself from asking about her ex Safaree Samuels, who appears on "Love & Hip Hop," a reality television series about the music industry, and if she would ever give Drake a shot. (I restrain myself greatly.) I don't know that anyone but her inner circle knows who Nicki Minaj really is.

This elusiveness is compounded by her fascinating catalog of performative alter egos, including Harajuku Barbie (a fashionista obsessed with pink and Minaj's longest-running persona), Nicki Teresa (known as "The Healer") and the sexually explicit Nicki Lewinsky — there is even a male persona, Roman Zolanski, a slightly exaggerated version of Minaj herself. She has a vocal range that can go from a high-pitched twittering to a growl in a few bars. In both music and regular conversation, she enjoys playing with accents, offering up valley girl-speak or island patois. During our time together, she switched to a British accent a couple of times and then effortlessly returned to her normal voice, a slightly affectless cadence that recalls her Queens upbringing. In public, she often wears dramatic makeup, dramatic outfits and a rainbow of dramatic wigs, which is to say she performs both on- and offstage. There is no point during our conversation where Minaj demonstrates anything but absolute self-awareness.

She pauses briefly before she answers my questions, as if calculating every possible outcome to everything she says. By the end of the interview, I am impressed by her fierce intelligence.

But she's at her most animated and unguarded when she's talking about music, and she thinks about music in deep and complex ways. She has strong opinions on what's necessary to make a great rapper: "Do you sound intelligent? Does your flow switch up? Are you in command of the beat? I listen for things like that." Jay-Z, Lil Wayne, Foxy Brown — "Those are the three I keep in my head when I'm writing because they've influenced me so much," she says. "I feel like I'm a part of all of them."

I'm curious about whom Minaj thinks she's influenced herself. She tells me that around two years ago, Kanye West said to her, " 'Every girl I hear rap, I can hear Nicki in her rap.' I didn't ask him who, but that was such a great compliment. Because sometimes you think you're the only one that can hear those types of things."

It feels like Minaj is on the verge of another big moment in her career, and she knows it. "This is definitely the most inspired and free and excited I've been since I started releasing albums through a label," she says. She is also deeply reflective about her evolution as an artist. I ask if the transition from making mixtapes to studio albums compromises the joy of creation and she answers, "Yeah, because ... artists do it to themselves. I'm not going to blame a label. You just overthink. When you're doing your own little thing, you feel like, I can be myself, I can be crazy. When you start working with a record company, you start thinking you need a bigger sound. I wanted to get back to the place where I wasn't second-guessing things so much. Sometimes simple is O.K."

I ask her what it has taken to get to this place of newfound confidence and trusting her instincts. "I believe in my gift wholeheartedly," she says. But this self-assurance was not easy to come by. "Sometimes I wake up and say, 'I don't know if I can do this anymore,' you know? I've had those times. I've had those years where I'm just like, 'Am

I good enough?'" But she believes in her "ability to withstand what would break the normal girl," she says.

At this point in her career, Minaj is able to reconcile, somewhat, her struggles. "I kind of love that I've had to go through so many hurdles to get where I am because I feel like I deserve it." She is frank about what she has been up against. "I had so much going against me in the beginning: being black, being a woman, being a female rapper. No matter how many times I get on a track with everyone's favorite M.C. and hold my own, the culture never seems to want to give me my props as an M.C., as a lyricist, as a writer. I got to prove myself a hundred times, whereas the guys that came in around the same time as I did, they were given the titles so much quicker without anybody second-guessing."

I am struck by these words because I've heard similar sentiments from other successful women in male-dominated industries — this sense that their endurance and perseverance contribute to their greatness. But, above all, Minaj has persevered because she is always in control of her craft. Neither her work nor her success are accidental. When we finish talking and I make my exit, there are more people in the hallway, waiting for their time with her. She remains in command of the beat.

CHAPTER 3

# Kendrick Lamar

Hailing from Compton, Calif., Kendrick Lamar's career has
been widely celebrated since his debut in 2004. He is
known for his musical inventiveness and politically charged
lyrics, epitomized in his multi-Grammy-winning 2015
album "To Pimp a Butterfly." Ryan Coogler, the director of
Marvel's "Black Panther," hired Kendrick to produce and
curate the film's highly regarded soundtrack. In 2018, he
became the first hip-hop artist to win the Pulitzer Prize for
Music for his record "DAMN."

## Kendrick Lamar, Emboldened, but Burdened, by Success

BY JON CARAMANICA | MARCH 17, 2015

CALLING MAINSTREAM HIP-HOP a series of compromises is unfair, but the
genre is far from where it was even a decade ago. It's still a privileged
space for black expression, but has also become extremely conscious
of everyone else listening in. Broadly speaking, it has reframed its
concerns as universal, not specific. It is, by and large, polite — a warm
and welcoming host.

Which is why Kendrick Lamar is the most ornery of modern rap
stars. His concerns are personal, local, interior. He prefers narratives
to anthems, verses to choruses, intricate feelings to intricate rhymes
(though he has those, too).

And yet despite those things — or maybe because of them — he has
fashioned a following, and a huge one at that — one that could make
him a potential change agent for the whole genre. His 2012 major label

debut album, "good kid, m.A.A.d. city," a long read about growing up in Compton, Calif., sold more than a million copies, a rare platinum hip-hop album in parched times, an exceptional exception.

That album's success has weighed on Mr. Lamar, and also emboldened him. His follow up, "To Pimp a Butterfly" (TDE/Aftermath/ Interscope), which in a surprise was released just before midnight on Sunday — is more brazen, more preoccupied with social politics and more revealing about the struggles of Mr. Lamar, the adult. It's a work about living under constant racialized surveillance and how that can lead to many types of internal monologues, some empowered, some self-loathing.

"Loving you is complicated," Mr. Lamar intones 10 times at the beginning of "u," a song in which he pillories himself for mistakes he has made during his rise. On "Mortal Man," he warns, "As I lead this army, make room for mistakes and depression." On "How Much a Dollar Cost," he tells a story about blowing off a beggar who, at the song's end, reveals himself to be God.

So Mr. Lamar is an imperfect warrior for change. But he has been agonizing over this role for years, long before the burden truly fell on his shoulders. In 2011, he was featured on "Buried Alive (Interlude)," on Drake's album "Take Care." His verse was meandering and paranoid, a young rapper tasting the spoils available to him and unsure whether to dig in or recoil in disgust.

Somehow, in "To Pimp a Butterfly," he does both. The album takes on bold, huge themes, reflective of Mr. Lamar's increasing confidence and increasing dissatisfaction. It's about ethics and community responsibility, about white terror and black resilience, about self-doubt and self-punishment, about melting under the klieg lights of fame.

At its best, it's a howling work of black protest art on par with Amiri Baraka's incendiary play "Dutchman," or David Hammons's moving decapitated hoodie "In the Hood" (seen most recently on the cover of Claudia Rankine's poetry collection "Citizen: An American Lyric") — works rooted in both pride and fear.

On "For Free? (Interlude)," he's indignant, lashing out at a society that gave him only the barest essentials and dared him to thrive: "Like I never made ends meet eatin' your leftovers and raw meat." On "The Blacker the Berry," he returns time and again to a wounded question — "You hate me, don't you?" — and calls out the structures of power that suggest that black lives don't matter:

*It's evident that I'm irrelevant to society*
*That's what you're telling me, penitentiary would only hire me*
*Curse me till I'm dead*
*Church me with your fake prophesizing that I'ma be just another slave*
*in my head*

Mr. Lamar has at best been a reluctant star, and also the rare artist who has become more interesting while in the crucible of fame, who hasn't smoothed out his rough edges. He likes playing characters: On "Institutionalized," he takes on the role of a friend who, when exposed to the new world Mr. Lamar has access to, tries to capitalize on it. And he likes bending his voice into unexpected shapes: On "u," he raps in a scarred, cracking voice, between tears and aggression.

While he has paved the way for the resurgence of Compton as a creative hotbed, with rappers like YG and Vince Staples making nouveau gangster rap, he is heavy with the burdens of yesterday. Ancestors hover over this album — Dr. Dre as life coach on "Wesley's Theory" ("Anybody can get it/The hard part is keeping it"); Snoop Dogg as the Slick Rick-like narrator of "Institutionalized"; and Tupac Shakur, resurrected for an eerie mock interview on "Mortal Man."

Musically, this album is a jolt of the old. Make no mistake, it is a jolt. It's full of neo-soul, regular old soul, jazz and funk, and the songs bubble with a furious spontaneity. There are implicit nods to J. Dilla, as on "Complexion (A Zulu Love)," which also features the classicist Pete Rock. The scrambling saxophones on "u" — by Terrace Martin, Kamasi Washington and Adam Turchin — are rousing. They continue on the next song, "Alright," produced partly by Pharrell Williams, and the closest thing this album has to a traditional single. (It has the faintest echo of Clipse's "When the Last Time.")

Mr. Lamar has always been a fluent technician, if an insular and anomic presence. But the increase in musicality around him has reshaped him. In the past, he has sometimes sounded as if he was rapping at the beat, not on it. But he's more comfortable in his pockets now.

There are several times when he veers into spoken-word territory on this album, a reminder that although aesthetics matter more here than on any prior effort by Mr. Lamar, he'll still look past them when trying to make a point.

He hasn't outrun his tendency toward clutter. He is a dense rapper, and even though he's more at ease with the music now, he still runs the risk of suffocation. He has also crammed "To Pimp a Butterfly" full: It totals 79 minutes, just shy of a typical CD's maximum capacity. It is a test, or a reflection of Mr. Lamar's faith in his followers.

Even though he memorably took on his hip-hop peers in 2013, on his verse on Big Sean's "Control, " the moments on this album in which he casts aspersions at other rappers feel unnecessary. That's because "To Pimp a Butterfly" is bigger than any minor intra-rapper friction. An album that asks questions as big as this one does, and that will be heard by so many, is a huge taunt to Mr. Lamar's peers — it's a dare to ride along, a dare to be different, a dare to be great.

# Kendrick Lamar, Hip-Hop's Newest Old-School Star

BY LIZZY GOODMAN | JUNE 25, 2014

"EVERYBODY JUST wants to have fun, be with the scene," Kendrick Lamar said when we met in his cramped quarters inside the Barclays Center in Brooklyn last fall. "Certain people get backstage, people that you would never expect.... You ain't with the media! You ain't into music! You ain't into sports! You're just here." The rapper, now 27, had just finished his set as the opening act on this stretch of Kanye West's Yeezus tour, and he was sitting low in an armchair in his trademark black hoodie surrounded by exactly those people.

"Hey, man, thank you again, appreciate the access back here, it means a lot to us," said an eager photographer who had overstayed his welcome. There was a knock on the door. "Hold up a minute, baby," Lamar's bodyguard, Big Mingo, said to a woman outside.

"We got iTunes out here," he said, turning to Lamar.

"She can come in," Lamar replied, waving her in.

By all appearances, there was a convivial party going on in his room, but the vibe was actually tense. There were two layers of conversation. The first layer was a loud and garish stream of talk, requests mostly — to play a festival, to come to a friend's club later that night — that came from acquaintances acting as intimates. The second layer was a series of subtle glances, exchanged among Lamar's people, aimed at gracefully minimizing how much time the rapper had to spend with each visitor. Eventually Lamar nodded to his manager, signaling that it was time to get the car. The previous evening, he stayed up all night working on new music, and he planned to do the same now.

As arrangements were being made to leave, he quietly told me, "As a kid, I used to stutter." It felt like an oddly personal line of conversation to begin amid the chaos, but because so many people were talking at him, no one else heard him. "I think that's why I put my energy into making music," he continued. "That's how I get my thoughts out, instead of being crazy all the time."

In the world of hip-hop, Lamar is widely considered to be a future king. Last year, he was nominated for seven Grammys, four of them for his 2012 major-label debut, "good kid, m.A.A.d city," which sold more than a million copies in the United States. His lyrical style and his background (Compton, Calif., born and raised) have shaped his reputation as the kind of old-school rapper you don't see much anymore, a street poet who has earned the affection of hip-hop purists as well as younger listeners. "He's the first person in a long time that a lot of the old heads respect," says the filmmaker and author Nelson George, one of the first journalists to write about rap music. "They see him as a real hip-hop M.C."

Part of what sets Lamar apart is pure lyrical agility. The producer and songwriter Pharrell Williams has likened Lamar to Bob Dylan. "He's a singer-songwriter," Williams says. "You can just see the kid's mind like a kaleidoscope over a beat." Lamar does indeed have a Dylan-like ability to pivot from playful to mystical, to reframe quotidian details as profound revelations, and he has an instinct for swirling, rhapsodic metaphor. He opens the track "Hol' Up" with this couplet: "I wrote this record while 30,000 feet in the air/Stewardess complimenting me on my nappy hair." A few verses later, he raps: "I lived my 20s at 2 years old, the wiser man, truth be told, I'm like 87/wicked as 80 reverends in a pool of fire with devils holding hands."

In person, Lamar is so serene and warm, and on his record, so erudite and philosophical, that it's tempting to read him as a mellow, cerebral guy, a monk reincarnated as a young rap star. But that would be a mistake. Lamar has made his name in part by trying to reawaken what George calls rap's "combative" energy, which has always been central to the genre's identity but has fallen off in the past decade.

"If my edge is dull, my sword is dull, and I don't want to fight another guy whose sword is dull," Lamar later told me. "If you've got two steel swords going back and forth hitting each other, what's gonna happen? Both of them are going to get sharper." He laments what he sees as the impotency that has taken over the rap game. "Everybody that's in the industry has lost their edge," he said. "There's really no aggression. You gotta say things particular, and everything is so soft." Last August, in a guest appearance on "Control," a track by Big Sean, Lamar named himself, alongside Jay-Z, Nas, Eminem and Outkast's Andre 3000, as the best M.C.s of all time. He also called himself "the king of New York" (a big no-no for a West Coast rapper) and sent out a message to his immediate peers: "I got love for you all, but I'm tryna murder you niggas/Tryna to make sure your core fans never heard of you niggas/They don't wanna hear not one more noun or verb from you niggas." The influential hip-hop magazine XXL called it "the verse that woke up the rap game."

Lamar approaches his music career with the ambition of an exacting, if sedate, C.E.O. At one point, after he left his Barclays Center dressing room, the crew descended on the catering table, eagerly assembling double-decker sandwiches and raiding the fridge for leftover Gatorade. "I've never been on a tour where there's no booze," someone grumbled. "I need alcohol." When I was on the road with Lamar, he didn't drink, and in general, his crew followed suit. This is part of his commitment to staying focused on his singular ambition: greatness. "There's a certain hunger that you can sense about Kendrick," Eminem says. "He raps to be the best rapper in the world. He competitive-raps. That's one of the things that's going to drive his career. He's going to be around for a long time."

"Will you hand me one of those Lunchables?" Lamar asked Matt Gant, a member of his crew who had opened one of the snack packs stacked in the minifridge backstage. The rapper had just finished his set at the Verizon Center in Washington. He sat on a rough brown couch wearing his standard postshow outfit: gray Nike sweatsuit, white athletic socks, Air Jordan sandals. West, who at 37 is 10 years older than Lamar, was onstage. Every so often, the bass from the multimillion-dollar sound system vibrated the dressing room's cheap-looking ceiling tiles, sending bits of dust cascading onto the catering table. A documentary on fracking played on a small TV bolted to the wall. "I ate so much of this in Europe, dawg, I got burned up," Lamar said, staring at his food. "I didn't want to see another Lunchable for a long time." Dave Free, Lamar's manager and one his best friends from home, entered, wearing a stylish wool baseball jacket and hat. "Uh oh," Free said, taking in the ennui of the assembled crew, which included Lamar's two bodyguards, a videographer and Gant. He lunged at Gant, smacking the Lunchable tray out of his hands. Shiny pink discs of processed turkey flew across the room. Everybody looked up from their phones, stunned. "That's some high-school [expletive] right there," Lamar said, chuckling.

"I had to do it," Free replied, shaking his head. "I'm so bored."

Some day Lamar may enjoy his own version of West-like dominance, but for now he was here, dodging lunchmeat grenades and ducking behind an ugly couch to change into new underwear straight out of the package. It was an honor to be on this tour, but it was also a drag. It meant flying back and forth between the coasts twice in the next 72 hours so he could perform at the American Music Awards without missing the Yeezus stop at Madison Square Garden and spending those long plane rides writing new raps with his thumbs on an iPhone. It also meant letting someone else dictate his schedule, while managing the already intense pressure to follow up the year-old "good kid, m.A.A.d city" with something even better.

Great records are great for different reasons. Some, like West's eclectic masterpiece, "My Beautiful Dark Twisted Fantasy," or Radiohead's "OK Computer," say, Look what I can do. Others, like "John Lennon/Plastic Ono Band" or Liz Phair's "Exile in Guyville" say, This is who I am. Lamar's "good kid, m.A.A.d. city" falls squarely into the who-I-am category. The album recasts his life growing up in the 'hood as a universal experience. One writer likened "good kid" to James Joyce's "Ulysses," because it uses detailed, interior language and a day in the life of one person to explore broader existential themes

was immediate: "One particular young lady," he said, referring to Alford. "She's been here since Day 1."

He's also clearly very close to his mother. Still stuck backstage at the Garden, Lamar tried to get her on the phone. She had been difficult to reach in L.A., and it was bothering him. "You're the worst with your phones!" he admonished after she finally picked up. "Dave's gonna come over there and drop off some clothes," he said, referring to Free, whom Lamar has dispatched to look after her.

If you're a fan of Lamar's music, you know his mother's voice. "Kendrick, where you at? I'm sittin' here waitin' on my van," she says during one of a series of snippets of real voice mail messages the rapper used as breaks in between songs on his album. "You told me you was gonna be back in 15 minutes. I gotta go the county building … I gotta get them food stamps!" Soon his father's voice comes in. "Is that Kendrick on the phone? … Hello? Yeah, where my [expletive] Domino's at?!" It's an authentic portrait, Lamar told me. "I could put them on the phone right now, and they'll sound exactly like that album."

His parents are originally from Chicago. "They came to L.A. on some …" Lamar paused. "Some high hopes. They had like $500. They landed in Compton out of every place in L.A.; I don't know how. They could have landed in the suburbs or the valley, but they didn't." It was the '80s, the height of the crack epidemic in America. "My pop did what he had to do," the rapper says of his father's profession, which he explicitly leaves unnamed. In the past, though, Lamar has said that his uncles ran drugs out of the project apartments in which he lived as a boy. "We had good birthdays and good Christmases. I can't complain." The "good kid, m.A.A.d city" album artwork features a photograph of Lamar's dad holding a shotgun. When he was growing up, Lamar said, "everybody that I touched physically, they ended up dead or in jail." That includes one of his younger brothers, who was incarcerated, he told me last fall. "I remember him saying, like, he wanted to be the hardest gang member; that's what he wanted to be," Lamar said, shaking his head.

It wasn't that Lamar didn't see the appeal of gang life. He was fired from the one real job he ever had, security at a truck stop, because his bosses suspected that he and his friends were planning to cause trouble. "I started thinking crazy, and the homies got in my head," he remembered. But he wasn't sold on the idea that gangs were the way to true brotherhood. "It's power," he said of what drew in his brother and so many others. "It's the sense of being wanted or being needed. Being in the gang, it's a certain type of love that you feel at the moment." Until, he said, things got real.

It helped, of course, that Lamar is quiet and gentle by nature, a self-described "observer." It helped even more that he had a father at home. "Fathers are not there a lot, and Kendrick's dad was no-nonsense," recalls Regis Inge, Lamar's former teacher, a veteran of the Compton school system who, the rapper told me, taught him poetry and how to write (they still play basketball when Lamar is home). And it especially helped that the young Lamar had a gift, already evident in his preteen years. "He was just better, and everybody knew that," Free remembered of Lamar's years as a student at Centennial High School, then a center of the local after-school freestyle-rap scene. "It got to the point when nobody wanted to rap with him. They were like, 'Yo, I'm gonna do my own thing.' " As a young teenager, wherever Lamar went — the cafeteria, the quad, the gym — he saw a potential audience and an opportunity to vie for the things all young men want: social power, influence and respect, plus attention from girls. "That is the No. 1 motivation when you are in ninth grade," Lamar said with a chuckle.

Lamar says his innate suspicion of convenient alliances and his resistance to temptation is just as handy now as it was then. "At 16, temptation can be money: I know money, I want money. Or women: I know women, I want women. Or drugs: I know drugs, I want drugs. Temptation is just the feeling that you're the most independent person on planet Earth. That you know everything." He continued: "That's something that we all go through as a kid. Now, this lifestyle that I'm in, the same thing exists! But it's 10 times worse, because everything is at my disposal. When you're in the limelight, you can get anything you want."

He was 16 when he put out his first mixtape, "Youngest Head Nigga in Charge," which got the attention of a prominent local manager, Anthony Tiffith, who goes by Top Dawg. Tiffith helped Lamar hone his skills, make connections within the underground hip-hop community and eventually founded Top Dawg Entertainment with Lamar as a key act. In 2010, the rapper's fourth mixtape, "Overly Dedicated," made an appearance on the Billboard hip-hop and R&B charts. It also caught the attention of Paul Rosenberg, who manages Eminem and has a long-standing relationship with Dr. Dre. Rosenberg got Lamar's music to Dre, who as a solo artist, producer and scout of new talent like Snoop Dogg, Eminem and 50 Cent, has become one of the most influential and well-respected figures in the music industry. He was impressed with Lamar and name-checked the young rapper in a local radio interview. "You hear Dr. Dre is supporting a young M.C. out in L.A., you're like, 'Oh, who the hell is that?' " Nelson George says. By 2011, Lamar and Dre were partners; there's a joint venture deal in place for Lamar's music between Top Dawg Entertainment and Dre's own label, an Inter-scope Records subsidiary called Aftermath Entertainment. Dre also makes two guest appearances on "good kid, m.A.A.d city."

Back at the Garden, word finally came over the walkie-talkies that Jamie Foxx, et al., had settled in successfully, clearing Lamar's vans to leave. Everyone stood up. "I need some snacks for the road," Lamar said, pouring a bowl of cereal and shoving into his sweatpants pocket a stack of $2 bills a fan handed him backstage. "Real rappers walk down hallways with money hanging out of their pocket eating cereal," he called out cartoonishly, spooning bites of cereal into his mouth and grinning as he walked down the hallway to the service elevator. "Everybody knows that."

I had been shadowing Lamar on tour with West off and on for almost three weeks before I saw the two rappers in the same room. The tour had swept through the Southern states and headed West. We were in Texas on an unusually cold Saturday evening just after a record-setting snowstorm. Lamar was heading to the stage at Houston's Toyota Center. As he walked down the hallway, a black van pulled up, and West got out with Kim Kardashian. As the two men greeted each other, their respective posses fell back — except for Lamar's videographer and his counterpart in West's camp, both of whom acted as if this was the moment they'd been waiting for all tour. They traced a tight circle around the men, lenses open to capture every word of a conversation that lasted less than 30 seconds. The two rappers embraced, then Lamar paused, allowing West to proceed down the hallway first, before continuing to the stage to play his set.

It's tempting to imagine that tour partnerships between an established star and an up-and-comer result in lots of communal bonding. And of course sometimes they do. Bono has become famous for taking young bands out on the road with U2 and dispensing his so-called Bono Talk, a sermon on how to avoid the pitfalls of fame. Lamar knew people wanted to think this was happening between him and West, and he obliged within reason, dutifully explaining to journalists how much he was learning from West or telling an employee of his label who asked if they had been hanging out, "We haven't really got an off day yet to chill out, but that's the plan." But a mentor-mentee relationship wasn't what was expected or desired, and it certainly was not what was happening.

Backstage in Houston, Lamar was visited by Devon Anjelica, a D.J. who goes by Devi Dev and is an old friend of his. "Do you realize you're further solidified in pop culture now?" she told him. Anjelica was anticipating a rout at the Grammys (which, of course, was not to be). But she also seemed convinced of far greater mainstream success. "You're going to be an answer on Trivial Pursuit." As she went on, Lamar sat on the edge of the couch, munching contemplatively on a green apple. "We'll see," he finally said, getting up to toss out the core. "A lot of this is politics, you know? You gotta be a realist."

This is how it is with Lamar all the time — he is constantly engaging in a mental version of the literal gatekeeping Big Mingo was overseeing in Brooklyn the day we first met. Every thought ("You're going to win a bunch of Grammys") and every request ("Come to my club") is weighed in an ever-changing calculus designed to maximize success and maintain sanity. "Everybody can't take this lifestyle," Lamar said early on. "To put that pressure on somebody not made for it, they'll go crazy."

The next day, we were all on the bus en route from Houston to San Antonio for a concert at the AT&T Center. I made my way to the back, joining Lamar in his traveling studio. He likes to tuck himself away in small, dark spaces, and this one was perfect: It contained only a bed and a recording deck. Lamar typed on 2Teez's iPhone (where he stores some of his raps), while the same foreboding beat played over and over again on the computer, little bars pulsating on the screen in hypnotic unison. "I'm the worst," he eventually said, breaking the silence. "Whenever I get good news about anything … man, I guess I'm bad at receiving compliments." He stopped typing but didn't look up from the phone, his face all but obscured beneath his black hood. "Like yesterday with the nominations, things like that — it made me feel like I had to be in the studio because I had to do it, not again, but … . " He couldn't quite finish his thought. "It just bothers me," he said finally. "I don't want to be something that just comes and goes."

# Notes on the Hip-Hop Messiah

BY JAY CASPIAN KANG | MARCH 24, 2015

THE HIP-HOP MESSIAH is both real and not real. He — and with the possible exception of Lauryn Hill, it has always been a "he" — is real in the sense that every five years or so, whenever hip-hop feels too boring, or, worse, too corporate, an artist will be appointed as the spiritual future of the form.

But the hip-hop messiah is also a prospective title: When he's anointed, it's not for the work he's already done, but more for the work he should do. He must create something that feels as though it has grown organically out of his city, but that is at the same time universal. His work must feel political, but not overtly political. He should be an example and a savior to the young black people who listen to his music. It's an impossible role to inhabit — at least while the hip-hop messiah is alive.

A partial list of hip-hop messiahs and the approximate years of their reign:

Rakim – 1987-1990
Nas – 1994-1996
Biggie – 1995-
Tupac – 1993-
Eminem – 2000-2003 (with qualifications)
Kendrick Lamar – 2012-

Shortly after Kendrick Lamar released "good kid, m.A.A.d city," his 2012 major-label debut, he was anointed the latest in the line of hip-hop messiahs by the critics, enthusiasts and solemn ex-rappers who determine these things. Like Nas — a one-time messiah himself — Lamar, a scrawny 25-year-old from Compton, was a visual poet. You can see Compton — the burger stands, the lights of the police cruisers, the 405 freeway — in every track of "good kid, m.A.A.d.

city," just as you can see the dice games, project hallways and parks of Queensbridge in Nas's "Illmatic."

Like Tupac, Lamar could effortlessly juxtapose his feelings of worthlessness with a bravado that was magnetic, inspiring. His rapping was so virtuosic that he almost seemed bored by his own skill, trying out new styles just because he could during guest appearances on other M.C.s' albums. Most important, he had that rare blend of raw talent, empathy and confidence that made every song, no matter how sad, ring with the kind of hope that you felt as a knot in your chest. Nas, in his prime, had the talent, Tupac had the empathy, Rakim had the confidence. In Lamar's songs — like "Sing About Me, I'm Dying of Thirst," maybe the finest the form has ever produced — you could hear all three knocking together.

"good kid, m.A.A.d city" was not only nakedly emotional, but also unexpectedly self-aware, with Lamar probing what his inevitable celebrity might mean. On the track "m.A.A.d city," he raps:

*"If I told you I killed a nigga at 16, would you believe me?*
*Or see me to be innocent Kendrick you seen in the street*
*With a basketball and some Now and Laters to eat*
*If I mentioned all my skeletons, would you jump in the seat?*
*Would you say my intelligence now is great relief?*
*And say it safe to say that our next generation maybe can sleep*
*With dreams of being a lawyer or doctor, instead of a boy with a chopper."*

These lines laid the groundwork for Lamar's new album, "To Pimp a Butterfly." He anticipated his messiah status even before it was bestowed on him and pushed back against the social burden placed on artists who, by virtue of their talent, are expected to lift up their communities. At the same time, he acknowledged the reality of this responsibility.

In the final moments of the "good kid, m.A.A.d city" track "Real," we hear a phone message from Lamar's mother. "Tell your story to these black and brown kids in Compton," she says. "Let 'em know you was just like them, but you still rose from that dark place of violence becoming a positive person. But when you do make it, give back with your words of encouragement and that's the best way to give back to your city." In "m.A.A.d city," Lamar seems to imagine himself as the local bard, one who doesn't have to answer to the white world or the music industry. He doesn't seem to want a wider, ambassadorial role, doesn't want to be the artist whom white kids play for their parents — the rapper whose "intelligence" is a "relief."

On "To Pimp a Butterfly," Lamar steps into a new role, one that feels shaped, in part, by the burdensome expectations placed upon him as a hip-hop messiah. In some ways, this was inevitable — every anointed rapper eventually has to move away from the memories of childhood to tell other kinds of stories. But few have done it as abruptly, and with as sharp a move from the personal to the explicitly political.

The new album is a thicket of inspirational, historical references; you'll find critical race theory, George Clinton, Nelson Mandela, Richard Pryor, Exodus 14, respectability politics and six separate levels of meta-analysis about the meaning of Lamar's success and messiah status. It seems almost designed for parsing in a college classroom. As Clover Hope pointed out in an excellent essay for Jezebel, the accumulation of all these black references washing over the listener creates its own mood, its own emotional timbre. But what you won't find on "To Pimp a Butterfly" are the engaging storytelling and descriptive eye that brought Lamar's Compton to life on "good kid, m.A.A.d. city."

In the song "Mortal Man," Lamar returns to, and updates, the questions he asked his fans in "m.A.A.d city":

*"Do you believe in me? Are you deceiving me?*
*Could I let you down easily, is your heart where it need to be?*
*Is your smile on permanent? Is your vow on lifetime?*
*Would you know where the sermon is if I died in this next line?*
*If I'm tried in a court of law, if the industry cut me off*
*If the government want me dead, plant cocaine in my car*

*Would you judge me a drug kid or see me as K. Lamar*
*Or question my character and degrade me on every blog*
*Want you to love me like Nelson, want you to hug me like Nelson*
*I freed you from being a slave in your mind, you're very welcome*
*You tell me my song is more than a song, it's surely a blessing*
*But a prophet ain't a prophet til they ask you this question:*
*When s— hits the fan, is you still a fan?"*

The distance between these questions and the ones Lamar asked in "m.A.A.d city" reveals his expanding ambitions, and also how those ambitions have changed. He is no longer heeding his mother's call to tell his story "to these young black and brown kids from Compton"; instead, he's become more interested in embracing the long history of black storytelling. The local bard, it seems, has left home.

"To Pimp a Buttefly" is a pilgrimage into blackness, but it's also a pilgrimage back into the idea of Lamar-as-hip-hop messiah. At the end of "Mortal Man," Lamar finally steps out of his dense thicket of references for a conversation between himself and Tupac. (Reviving Tupac has become its own odd industry in recent years. This exhumation was done by taking audio of an interview Tupac gave two years before his death in 1996 and splicing it together with Lamar's new interjections.) They talk about the limits of black strength, the possibility of revolution and the exhaustion of young black men. Lamar asks Tupac what he thinks of the future of Lamar's generation.

"It's gonna be murder," Tupac says. "It's gonna be like Nat Turner, 1831, up in this mother—, you know what I'm saying. It's gonna happen."

"That's crazy, man," Lamar says. "In my opinion, the only hope we kinda have left is music. Vibrations."

This is the closest "To Pimp a Butterfly" comes to clarity. If, as Lamar tells Tupac, music is the only hope left and "vibrations" are the key, the experimentation found on "To Pimp a Butterfly"could be seen as a spray of different frequencies. And yet even the conversation feels conceptual and referential — Lamar mostly defers to Tupac and ends the exchange with an extended metaphor that helps explain the title of the album. The excitement you feel while listening to it comes from the idea of the two talking, not from what's actually said. And while there's no quarter or equivocation on Tupac's end, you can't help but wish Lamar had more to say than "That's crazy."

Over the past few days, I've listened to "To Pimp a Butterfly" at home, on the train, on a plane, while eating dinner and while watching a basketball game at night. Each time, when I start feeling bored or listless, I'll stare down at my phone and try to find the one track that will snap me back to attention. On "Illmatic," it was "Memory Lane" or "Life's a Bitch." On Notorious B.I.G.'s "Ready to Die," it was "Warning" or "Suicidal Thoughts." On "good kid, m.A.A.d city," it was "Sing About Me, I'm Dying of Thirst." There isn't a track like that on "To Pimp a Butterfly." And while the album was clearly intended as something more than a collection of iTunes singles, it is disappointing that a work with so much musical complexity lacks the emotional texture of "good kid, m.A.A.d city." Part of the considerable genius of that album lies in how effortlessly Lamar weaves together the careless fun of "Backseat Freestyle" and the despair of "I'm Dying of Thirst" into a seamless story of one day in Compton. This album is the opposite. It's effortful, with a touch of piety.

Many of the first critical responses to "To Pimp a Butterfly" pleaded for more time to figure out what, exactly, Lamar was doing. In Slate, Carl Wilson wrote, "It's too soon to say whether 'To Pimp a Butterfly' is a more satisfying album." In The Fader, Rawiya Kameir wrote, "God knows how long it will be before any of us fully grasp the stacked meanings, extended metaphors and shrouded complexities of Kendrick Lamar's 'To Pimp a Butterfly.' Definitely weeks, probably months." There seemed to be a reluctance, especially among white critics, to straightforwardly criticize the album. ("How should white listeners approach the 'overwhelming blackness' of Kendrick Lamar's brilliant new album?" read the deferential subheadline to Wilson's review.) This caution is a testament to Lamar's talent, but also to the power that comes with his messiah status: Critics seem afraid to say much about this album because they want to believe in him too, even when what's in front of them doesn't exactly deliver on their expectations.

Lamar, himself, might not quite know what he has created. There is a hoarder's mania to this album — he seems to have gathered every idea and influence he could find without too much care for what all that clutter reveals, knowing only that there is something beautiful in it. When he homes in on what exactly that is, hip-hop will have another classic. Until then, we will have to be satisfied with watching him make an exciting but still-unfinished transition.

Which is just as well. Not every album needs to feel like it was handed down from the mount. The ones that try to are usually either a mess of shoddy uplift and shoddy politicking (Nas's "It Was Written") or inward-facing rage (Eminem's "The Marshall Mathers LP"). There's a hint of both in "To Pimp a Butterfly," and while Lamar's talent and thoughtfulness elevate him clear of those sorts of misfires, the problem with messiah status is that it converts all of its holders, whether they come from Queensbridge, the Bronx, Atlanta or Compton, into the same figure. Like the best narrative poets, Lamar has a genius for wringing uncommon emotion out of highly wrought verse. The hip-hop messiah, by contrast, will always be antipersonal.

**JAY CASPIAN KANG** is a contributing writer for The New York Times Magazine.

# Kendrick Lamar, Rapper Who Inspired a Teacher, Visits a High School That Embraces His Work

BY COLLEEN WRIGHT | JUNE 8, 2015

WHEN BRIAN MOONEY'S students struggled in March to digest the literary themes and dense language in Toni Morrison's novel "The Bluest Eye," Mr. Mooney sought inspiration from an unorthodox teacher of his own: the two-time Grammy winner and world-famous rapper Kendrick Lamar.

Mr. Mooney, who teaches freshman English at High Tech High School in North Bergen, N.J., played Mr. Lamar's album (edited, of course) "To Pimp a Butterfly" to draw correlations to Ms. Morrison's novel.

Using a literary lens called "hip-hop ed" that he learned during his graduate courses at Teachers College at Columbia University, Mr. Mooney asked his students to reflect on the dichotomy of black culture in America — the celebration of itself and its struggle with historic oppression. His students' sudden understanding shined through essays, colorful canvases and performance art.

Mr. Mooney, 29, blogged about his curriculum and shared his students' work online. The blog racked up over 10,000 Facebook shares, and hardly a month passed before Mr. Lamar discovered it.

On Monday, Mr. Lamar not only became a guest lecturer in Mooney's small classroom at High Tech, but he also became a pupil. Mr. Lamar's manager sent a note to Mr. Mooney in April saying the performer was interested in visiting. He did not charge a fee, but the school and its foundation paid for the stage setup.

"I was feeling incredibly grateful and humbled that my work received that much exposure and reached that wide of an audience that Kendrick himself read it," Mr. Mooney said.

The hip-hop artist Kendrick Lamar, at right in gray shirt, in a poetry slam Monday at High Tech High School in North Bergen, N.J.

The administration at High Tech High School, a magnet school, embraced Mr. Lamar's visit. Mr. Mooney packed about 50 of his students from his world literature freshman class, after-school hip-hop literature class and extracurricular slam poetry club, for a session with Mr. Lamar.

Selected students performed spoken word sessions and raps for Mr. Lamar. "You've chose the wrong butterfly to pimp," spat Alejandro Leon, a 15-year-old, paying homage to Mr. Lamar's album. Mr. Lamar praised Mr. Leon's poem with finger snaps and complimented his punch lines. Even Mr. Mooney showed off his rapping skills, and Mr. Lamar's head bobbed to the beat.

"Man, this is a blast," Mr. Lamar, 27, told the class. "I can see the energy. I can feel the energy."

The class discussed the inspiration behind Mr. Lamar's albums and his perception as an author himself. Mr. Lamar signed students' artwork along the classroom walls and took selfies with beaming students.

"When I talk to kids, I'm really listening," he said. "When I do that, we have a little bit of a bigger connection than me being Kendrick Lamar and you being a student. It's almost like we're friends. Because a friend listens."

The class joined the rest of the student body, about 650 in total, in the school's field house. Mr. Lamar sat on a panel with Chris Emdin, Mr. Mooney's mentor from Teachers College and creator of the #hiphoped movement; Jamilia Lyiscott, who recently received a Ph.D. from Teachers College; Mr. Mooney; and some High Tech alumni to critique performances by the students.

Sade Ford, an 18-year-old senior, took the stage with her performance titled "It Takes a Village to Raise a Butterfly." She touched upon leaving behind her hometown, Jersey City, and her coming journey as a first-generation college student at Rutgers University.

"The best part is the effect that she can give her perspective from different walks of life," Mr. Lamar commented.

Another senior, Benjamin Vock, 17, created his poem within a day, inspired by Mr. Lamar's song "Mortal Man." He bemoaned the pain the black community felt with the deaths of young black men such as Michael Brown and Trayvon Martin and the privilege he experienced growing up white.

"That's dope," Mr. Lamar said. "You identify with my community and what's going on in the world. And I appreciate you for that."

To close out his visit, Mr. Lamar took a single song request. He settled on a performance of "Alright."

"It's truly a blessing to be in front of you all," Mr. Lamar signed off. "I will be back. That's a promise, y'all."

# The Blacker the Berry

BY MARLON JAMES | MARCH 10, 2016

NEARLY EVERY RAP ALBUM has that one moment you can't get with. If you're a woman, there are at least five. It's been almost a year since I first heard Kendrick Lamar's "To Pimp a Butterfly," an ambitious, spellbinding, masterpiece of a rap album, and it took me nearly a year to like it. The main reason: the 13th song, "The Blacker the Berry." Up to that moment, musically if not lyrically, "Butterfly" is almost a quiet storm of an album, a record that gazes more inward than out, even as it tackles institutional racism and hood politics. Then comes "The Blacker the Berry," all booming drums and NWA-style rage. For the first time, homeboy is furious, as if he has just realized that the only response to the stereotype of the angry black man is to get angrier. It's the part where I thought I would be most engaged, but it turned into the part that locked me out.

"Butterfly" arrived at an unprecedented moment in pop. Black artists, as they conquered the mainstream, were getting even blacker. Kanye might have gotten there first (at least he probably thinks so) with "New Slaves" and "Black Skinhead," and now even Beyoncé is place-checking New Orleans and image-checking the Black Panthers. But Kanye was still speaking to the white gaze, the hatred and desire in it, and taking revenge by getting all black-sex-machine on somebody's white wife. "Butterfly" is instead Toni Morrison circa "Sula": not looking outside for either validation or opposition. Black love, black empowerment, black history and black wisdom are explored so deeply and intelligently that you assume that conservative media fetish, black-on-black crime, will never show up. But then, in the third verse of "The Blacker the Berry," when Kendrick is waxing lyrical on Trayvon Martin's death, it does. All of a sudden "Blacker" becomes a song about black accountability while black men are being murdered and the implausible logic of slamming two ideas into the same thought. I was right there with him until that third verse.

You can't be a hip-hop head and not be hit by "The Blacker the Berry." It brings the boom-bap from the get-go, dropping funk on the one, like an update of the drum break that opens NWA's album "Straight Outta Compton." And even though I was tired of people's mapping anger onto blackness, Lamar's detonation of rage and wit was (and is) unmatched in hip-hop. He grabs at stereotypes as if they're slipping out of his fingers ("My hair is nappy," he says. "My nose is round and wide") and throws them right back at whoever would deploy them. He's not even rapping so much as spitting fire, jumping on a line, retracing it, firing it back at you, like the boxer Jack Johnson when he said: "I'm black, they never let me forget it. I'm black, all right, I'll never let them forget it." Kendrick fuels his "I'm black" with the knowledge that ain't a damn thing changed. He leaves it to the Jamaican DJ Assassin to bring backup in the chorus, drawing the line from plantation to street corner and the switch in who controls black self-determination, from the "whips left scars 'pon me back" to the "the big whip parked 'pon the block."

The second verse widens the focus and ups the power. Part of the thrill as a listener is hearing him go there, go further than anybody else. ("Church me with your fake prophesizing/that I'mma be just another slave in my head/Institutionalized manipulation and lies.") He takes church, the black community's own sacred cow, and minces it, turning the noun into a verb that means "to spread deceit." This is primo Kendrick, outside and inside at once, global and street, sometimes in the same line.

The last couplet on the second verse echoes the first, with a crucial change: "You sabotage my community, makin' a killin'/you made me a killer," turns into, "How can I tell you I'm making a killin'?/You made me a killer" — and the different spin on "killing" weighs a ton. In the first instance, exploitation and indifference make him a killer. In the second, his success comes from America's obsession with his assuming he looks like one. It was almost unbearable to anticipate what this prophet of rage was going to drop next.

And then he dropped it.

I could feel the verse pulling away from me as soon as he got half-way into it. It turned into call-and-response, me and this third verse, which went a little something like this:

*"It's funny how Zulu and Xhosa might go to war. ...*
*Remind me of these Compton Crip gangs that live next door."*

Me: Hold up, K-dot, what is this you're dropping? No, dude, those are two nations going to war. And fine, war is hell, but if Britain and France aren't called thugs for Waterloo, if Lancaster and York aren't called bangers despite literally being family killing family, then why do Zulu vs. Xhosa get compared to gang warfare? Because it weakened them both in the face of the real enemy? Either all war is hell, or all war is thuggery. I'm fine with either, but not with a special distinction when Africans do it.

Kendrick continues:

*"So don't matter how much I say I like to preach with the Panthers*
*Or tell Georgia State 'Marcus Garvey got all the answers'*
*Or try to celebrate February like it's my B-Day*
*Or eat watermelon, chicken and Kool-Aid on weekdays*
*Or jump high enough to get Michael Jordan endorsements*
*Or watch BET cause urban support is important*
*So why did I weep when Trayvon Martin was in the street*
*When gangbanging make me kill a nigga blacker than me?*
*Hypocrite!"*

Me: No, brother, no! Here was a black man invoking the detestable slogan of black-on-black crime to prevent himself from mourning the unjustifiable homicide of a black boy by a Neighborhood Watch vigilante. All I could think was: Where the hell was Kendrick going?

Things can get messy when the black gaze turns inward, to this thing called personal accountability. Personal responsibility. Personal respectability. Bootstrappism. The black man employing the despicable liberal "but," heralding a switch to victim-shaming. A woman has the right to wear what she wants, but. Black men can wear hoodies and let their pants sag, but. Rap has never been scared of being contrarian, and so here I thought that maybe he was deliberately playing with the idea, deliberately embodying the perspective to eventually show it up for what it was. Nas once wrote a song from the point of view of a gun. But then Kendrick of all people dropped a "but" himself, in a conversation with Billboard magazine right before the album's release.

"What happened to [Michael Brown] should've never happened," he said. "Never. But when we don't have respect for ourselves, how do we expect them to respect us? It starts from within. Don't start with just a rally, don't start from looting. It starts from within."

Kendrick wasn't the first, and he won't be the last, to make the statement that black deaths are in some way blacks' fault and that black lives might be a matter of personal responsibility, right down to clothing choice. The idea that a sudden dose of self-respect is part of what is needed to stop the police from killing us is not only ludicrous — Amadou Diallo wasn't a gangbanger, but he was shot at 41 times anyway; I think we can assume that the Rev. Martin Luther King Jr. had it all right within, but that didn't protect him from being brutalized by all sorts of authority, nor did his dressing impeccably prevent him from arrest — it is also old. It's a belief that the black person has a role to play in the erasure of hate toward herself. That kind of thinking almost suggests that racism makes sense.

But racism makes no sense. It is perverse and aberrant yet such a constituent part of the American make up, so normalized in all its forms, that it's no surprise that the black person would scramble for answers as to why it exists. And in scrambling for answers, you look everywhere, even within: Did I do something to bring this on? Was a part of this outcome in even the slightest way my fault?

Fact is, black people have always believed in respectability politics. It's also at the core of the non-American black's perspective on race, and I should know, because as a non-American black, I've traded in that belief for years. It's particularly acute with us Jamaicans. Our stories are everywhere: How despite racism, or rather the black American's self-destructive perception of it, we worked hard to excel and gain respect. We achieved. Everybody knows how hard we Jamaicans work. That's why I have that job and you, black American, do not. Maybe you should stop whining about your troubles and own up to your laziness. Maybe if you do what I did, you would be manager of that Chase branch on the corner, just like me.

Bootstrappism is the chocolate echo of white racism. You can find it in black self-help and how-I-became-a-millionaire books. Prince with "America," Ice Cube with "Look Who's Burning." Lauryn Hill berating black girls who get hair weaves to look like Europeans. Nearly every time Steve Harvey addresses black people. President Barack Obama telling Morehouse College students at their 2013 commencement that there's "no time for excuses," a lesson that the fact of their existence proved they didn't need. It's a road that leads to the granddaddy of the bootstrap, Bill Cosby, who declared in a 2004 speech that black kids were being shot because they were going around stealing Coca-Cola and poundcake.

I could feel the verse pulling away from me as soon as he got halfway into it.

But Kendrick's conclusion is far more sophisticated than anything Cosby has ever said. In fact, it's not a conclusion at all. It was Kendrick doing what he does better than anybody else: complicating a discussion at exactly the point where everybody, including me, tries to simplify it. And this is what he was aiming for all along, questioning what even many black people would never dare question, arguing that yes, every argument, even this one, has two sides. More sides. Adding layers we might need but don't want. And that's what he did next, not on wax, but on MTV.

"Know who I am first," he said. And then he said more than that:

"When I say, 'Gangbanging made me kill a nigga blacker than me,' this is my life that I'm talking about. I'm not saying you; you might not even be from the streets. I'm not speaking to the community, I'm not speaking of the community," he continued. "I am the community."

Fast-forward to near the end of 2015, and I'm on a flight to New York. Thirty thousand feet above everything, I put on "Butterfly," and something that never happened before happens. This incredible clarity, as if I'd been listening to the soul brother all year but only now was finally hearing him. And then I got to that song, No. 13, the sticking point, the one reason I hadn't been able to join the best-of-the-year showering of praise, and I realized something that felt sudden yet inevitable. That this song, with its booming beat, the loudest on the record, that seemed to herald it as some global political statement, was in fact Kendrick's most deeply personal. Almost implosive. That the moment wasn't about we at all, it just sounded that way. It's his most "I" moment, reflecting a reality that I couldn't possibly connect to, only witness and try to understand. It's as personal as Ice Cube's "Dead Homiez." He's not speaking to the community or for the community. He's speaking for himself or, rather, a version of himself. The smarter me looked in the mirror and asked: "Well, who's the one playing representational politics here? Who is the one expecting the black man to be Everyman, black man to reflect the universal good will, or at the very least a carefully curated black rage directed at a carefully identified target?"

Hip-hop has always been about spinning clever fictions, doing what great narratives do: inventing stories that tell the real truth. But post-Biggie and Tupac, it's so easy to fall hard for hip-hop's insistence on keeping it real that I'm surprised how easily I still fall for it, thinking that "Butterfly" is either confessional or reportage, when it's neither. We do this over and over, judging artists of color based on a warped idea that legitimacy can come only from experience. You would think I would know better, given that as a novelist, I deal with the same assumption in nearly every interview. One journalist even congratulated me for escaping the ghetto through "the power of the pen and not the gun."

My last novel was about Jamaican gang members manipulated by politicians into an attempt on Bob Marley's life. Young men, murderers before 15, murdered before 18. Nearly everybody assumed that I had experienced some of this. In fact, the first time I heard a live gunshot was watching Martin McDonagh's play "A Behanding in Spokane." And once each interviewer was convinced that there was no blood on my hands, then came the skepticism, the disbelief, the doubting: By what authority was I telling these stories? As if knowledge, talent and imagination weren't enough for a writer of color to make art; as if a work of art can't be personal and fictitious at the same time, invented and meaningful.

And here I was doing the same thing to Kendrick. He was just a man wondering how someone gets to be part of the Black Lives Matter conversation when black lives don't matter to him. How someone can feel rage at murder while being fine with suicide. He was exploring these themes as concepts — you know, that thing that artists do. He was posing tricky, difficult questions, for which there were no answers, getting into the middle of his song, feeling it, breathing it, but still inventing. I wonder how much of what I thought my problem was with "The Blacker the Berry" stemmed from me doing what is still being done to me: Questioning the black gaze, assuming that it must have sprung from something other than the storyteller's gift. That it must be autobiography or documentary. I've never listened to Radiohead's "A Wolf at the Door" and wondered if Thom Yorke ever paid ransom money for his kidnapped children. Or thought Johnny Cash ever murdered anybody or knew anyone who did. Just like those songs, "The Blacker the Berry" is several things at once, but mostly, at its essence, it's just that thing we call art.

**MARLON JAMES**, a novelist, is the 2015 recipient of the Man Booker Prize.

# Kendrick Lamar's Anxiety Leads to Joy and Jabs on New Album

REVIEW | BY JON CARAMANICA | APRIL 16, 2017

OF ALL THE CHARACTERISTICS that set Kendrick Lamar apart — his blazing verbal gifts, his determined cultural politics, his resolute aesthetic modesty — perhaps the most unusual, especially in this era of hyper-connectedness, has been his particular blend of assuredness and indifference. Excepting the occasional sidelong shot at a peer — one that's fired down from the top of the mount, really — it often sounds as if he needed to hear only his own ticktock for guidance.

But he has been listening all along, watching how others perceive him, feeling the shifts in their energy. That's the Mr. Lamar who shows up on the tart and punchy "DAMN.," his fourth studio album. This is a work of reactions and perceptions, a response to the sensations that come when the world is creeping in and you can't keep it at bay any longer without lashing back.

Two of the most striking examples of this recur throughout "DAMN." In one, Mr. Lamar samples Fox News commentators responding to his 2015 uplift anthem, "Alright," with derision, including Geraldo Rivera's suggesting that hip-hop is worse for black youth than racism (and Mr. Lamar addresses Mr. Rivera directly on "YAH.").

In the other, Mr. Lamar repeatedly laments that those close to him have forsaken him: "Aint nobody prayin' for me," he intones several times on "FEEL.," a sentiment he revisits elsewhere, and "FEAR." is driven home with the use of a voice-mail message from a cousin of Mr. Lamar's, who locates that feeling of isolation in biblical terms.

Taken in total, it's clear — for Mr. Lamar, there's nowhere to turn for trust, safety, peace.

And so on "DAMN." he's biting back, something that begins before the music even starts. The album and song titles are rendered in caps, with a period at the end. Defiant, controlled jabs. Exclamations without exclamation points. Mr. Lamar peers out from the album cover, focused and wary.

That continues on this sometimes boisterous, sometimes swampy, rarely fanciful album — it's Mr. Lamar's version of the creeping paranoia that has become de rigueur for midcareer Drake.

And yet this is likely Mr. Lamar's most jubilant album, the one in which his rhymes are the least tangled — on several songs, he returns to the same phrase, for emphasis — and his stories here are the most pointed. On "FEEL.," he's watching his carefully stacked walls of protection begin to crumble:

*I feel like friends been overrated*
*I feel like the family been faking*
*I feel like the feelings are changing*
*Feel like my daughter compromised and jaded*
*Feel like you wanna scrutinize how I made it*

He trudges a similar path on "PRIDE.," which begins with a harrowingly beautiful intro by Steve Lacy, of the group the Internet, which Mr. Lamar follows with a low, groaning flow as he details the misery of doubt:

*See, in the perfect world, I would be perfect, world*
*I don't trust people enough beyond they surface, world*
*I don't love people enough to put my faith in men*
*I put my faith in these lyrics, hoping I make amend*

Mr. Lamar's belief in music may well be the only faith left unshaken here. His songs limn classic Los Angeles gangster rap, but also that city's kinetically inventive progressive independent scene of the early-to-mid-1990s. He sprinkles in a couple of gestures to classic hip-hop, including a callback to the signature clipped cadence from Juvenile's "Ha" on "ELEMENT.," and the recurrent use of the celebrated New York mixtape DJ Kid Capri, whose excited yelps are peppered throughout. Mr. Lamar also recruits high-profile guests: There's a smooth collaboration with Rihanna, "LOYALTY.," and "XXX," which features some reassuringly understated singing by Bono, of U2.

"DAMN." is also a bit of an exhale after a few years of high-intensity balancing of social and aesthetic concerns. On "ELEMENT." Mr. Lamar reinforces that his concerns are interior, especially coming off his last album, "To Pimp a Butterfly" from 2015, which became a flash point for black political awareness and activism. "Last LP I tried to lift the black artists," he raps here, "But it's a difference 'tween black artists and wack artists."

And taunting — an underappreciated Kendrick Lamar skill — is the core of "HUMBLE.," one of the album's most fiery songs: "I don't fabricate it, most of y'all be fakin'/ I stay modest 'bout it, she elaborate it/This that Grey Poupon, that Evian." It's an approach he returns to often here, more than his usual knotty parables.

Well, there is one knotty parable: "DUCKWORTH.," the album's finale, which tells the apparently true story of how, decades ago, his label boss crossed paths with his father in near-violent fashion, in an incident that could have ended with bullets and tears. But everyone walked away unscathed: At least in one moment in time, in one specific place, someone was praying for Mr. Lamar.

# Kendrick Lamar, Rap's Skeptical Superstar, Avoids Arena Spectacle

REVIEW | BY JON CARAMANICA | JULY 13, 2017

GLENDALE, ARIZ. — In the last year, big-tent hip-hop concerts have taken to the skies, making the space above the arena floor as important as the stage. In 2016, Kanye West performed on a platform dangling perilously low above a moshing crowd, and Drake filled the empty arena air with a sinuous light show. Now stage diving is the thing, peaking in May when Lil Uzi Vert climbed to the top of a tower at a Miami festival and flew into a rapturous crowd.

In part, this reflects the rappers' outsized ambition and latent boredom with simple symbols of excess. Rather than become shinier, or more expensive, these concerts have become gaseous, expanding to fill the volume provided.

Kendrick Lamar, rap's most modest, skeptical and monastic superstar, is having none of that.

On Wednesday night, at the Gila River Arena in this northwestern Phoenix suburb, Mr. Lamar began his nationwide arena tour with a show that was far simpler than those of his peers: For the most part, one man on one stage, making the vast room feel tiny and intensely focused.

That has a lot to do with the nature of Mr. Lamar's art, which is anti-flamboyant, interior and complex. He is a blazing technical rapper and a relentless searcher, and as he has become more famous and successful, he hasn't backed away from those traits.

What's changed is how many people are watching. "DAMN.," Mr. Lamar's fourth studio album, released in April, is his first record rooted in the tensions associated with success. He leaned heavily on it at this concert, returning again and again to the album's most potent mantra: "Ain't nobody prayin' for me."

Kendrick Lamar was largely alone onstage, but he was backed by a live band that was out of view.

That declaration is one thing to say on an album, and another thing altogether when a crowd of about 18,000 is saying it back to you. The immersion was churchlike, less about sensory overload than a fervent commitment to take in a pastor issuing one demanding statement after another.

For all its self-interrogation, "DAMN." is Mr. Lamar's most accessible album, and the one in which he finally allows anthemic impulses to fully coexist with his at times ornery aesthetic. Songs like "DNA.," "LOYALTY." and "HUMBLE." had the gut-punch and abandon to rouse this arena, as did the older songs "Alright" and "Backseat Freestyle." Though Mr. Lamar was largely alone onstage, backed by an obscured-from-view live band, which made the reticent jazz-inflected soul he prefers to rap over into something denser, greasier and more shattering.

Throughout his hour-and-a-half set, Mr. Lamar was energetic and nimble — his body communicated joy, exasperation, supreme confidence. Sometimes his movements were herky-jerky, as if he were absorbing invisible blows. Rarely did he indulge in grand gestures (apart from a couple of deep bows as he took in some extended adulation from the audience). He was a worker with a job to do, and he did it without much glamour.

There were occasional pyrotechnics, some lighting rigs moving around the stage and, late in the show, a ceiling that descended until it hovered just over Mr. Lamar's head. On one song, he appeared to float horizontally, just above a dancer who was floating parallel beneath him. For a handful of songs, he rapped on a platform in the middle of the arena floor, sometimes in a low crouch. And at various points in the night, a lightly comedic kung fu film starring Mr. Lamar played on a screen behind him — it was the only time you could see him smile.

Mr. Lamar's set was a wild contrast with that of Travis Scott, who performed just before him, and is one of contemporary hip-hop's most energetic and disruptive live performers. Unlike Mr. Lamar's music, which is dense and Morse-code tricky, Mr. Scott's songs are psychedelic and woozy, and sometimes sound incomplete. But onstage, he is an entrancing maniac, and here, even more so given that he delivered half of his set from atop a huge bird that swooped up and down, left and right, over the main stage. (The other opener was the Virginia sing-rap jester D.R.A.M.)

If Mr. Scott was running an obstacle course, Mr. Lamar was engaged in calisthenics. His performance ranged from urgent cris de coeur to languorous meditations, but he delivered both with the same blue-collar virtuosity. And at the end of the show, after performing the incendiary "HUMBLE." twice, he returned for a two-song encore, the swampy "FEEL." and "GOD.," that was decidedly more muted. It was as if, after a night preoccupied with avoiding polish, he had spotted one rogue bit, and came out to scrape it away.

# Kendrick Lamar Gives 'Black Panther' a Weighty Soundtrack

REVIEW | BY JON PARELES | FEB. 14, 2018

ALL THE SYMBOLIC WEIGHT attached to "Black Panther" — as a major Hollywood blockbuster with an African superhero, an African-American director, a majority-black cast and a vision of a highly advanced, self-sufficient, colonialism-free African kingdom — extends to "Black Panther the Album," a collection of songs "from and inspired by" the film. That's a loose enough rubric to give the album's executive producers, Kendrick Lamar and the CEO of his label, Anthony Tiffith, known as Top Dawg, the leeway to build a coherent album that juggles multiple missions.

After four studio albums and many other releases, Mr. Lamar is this moment's pre-eminent rapper: furiously inventive, thoughtful, virtuosic, self-conscious, musically adventurous and driven. "Black Panther the Album" is very nearly as densely packed — with ideas, allusions and ambitions — as one of Mr. Lamar's official solo albums. He's superbly abetted by his frequent collaborator Sounwave (Mark Spears), the producer or co-producer on almost every track, who shifts the atmosphere constantly — often within a single song — deploying ratchety trap percussion, menacing electronics, blurry pitch-shifted samples, and even a rock guitar.

"Black Panther" does include the mandatory action-film pop anthems. In "All the Stars," Mr. Lamar raps about conflict between hopeful choruses from SZA. But the song's release as a single has been marred by complaints that its video clip imitates, without credit, the imagery of a Liberian-British artist, Lina Iris Viktor.

Ending the album is the more grimly determined "Pray for Me," with the Weeknd mournfully vowing to "spill this blood for you" and Mr. Lamar rapping about how "I fight the world, I fight you, I fight myself" over a track that vaguely suggests African drumming and

traditional ululations. Ballads, another soundtrack-album require-
ment, are equally burdened. The English songwriter Jorja Smith sings
"I Am" over an adamantly sluggish drumbeat and a lonely guitar line,
affirming a sense of duty: "When you know what you got, sacrifice
ain't that hard," she declares.

The album's broader strategy is to hint at the movie's story while
concentrating on tales of struggle and swagger much closer to home.
From the songs, it would be easy to believe the movie was set in California, although there are bits of African input tucked in.

Mr. Lamar dips into the roles of both T'Challa, the African king of
the fictitious Wakanda who is also the Black Panther, and Erik Killmonger, his tenacious adversary. Yet in the track "Black Panther,"
which ends with the words, "I am T'Challa," Mr. Lamar is also quite
insistently "King Kendrick": "King of the answer, king of the problem,
king of the forsaken," he raps over a nagging, dissonant loop. Later in
the track, with an almost conspiratorial voice, he asks, "What do you
stand for? Are you an activist?"

Mr. Lamar announces "All hail King Killmonger" in "King's Dead,"
after a litany of repudiation and denial — "Not your baby, not your
equal/Not the title y'all want me under" — that may sum up Killmonger's negativity. But it also parallels Mr. Lamar's refusal on his
albums to accept oversimplified roles like spokesman or generational
conscience.

The album's many guests don't try as hard to connect with the
movie. Most of them appear as California figures, flaunting fancy cars
and thinking about street-level battles. "Paramedic!" is a showcase for
the Sacramento group SOB X RBE, boasting about being "heavy in the
streets" over plinking percussion. Ab-Soul and Anderson .Paak share
"Bloody Waters," matter-of-factly describing growing up around, and
perpetuating, endless lethal gang rivalries: "It's warfare. Is war fair?
No.," Ab-Soul raps.

The album welcomes some South African rappers and singers, and
there are brief glimpses of South African rhythms; its most cheerfully

upbeat song, "Redemption," features the South African singer Babes Wodumo riding the South African club beat called gqom. Mr. Lamar and Vince Staples share "Opps" with Yugen Blakrok, a South African rapper as quick and convoluted in her boasts as they are: "Crushing any system that belittles us/Antidote to every poison they administer/ Switch it like time signatures," she raps. The track, produced by Sounwave with the composer of the film's orchestral score, Ludwig Göransson, uses a low, scowling synthesizer line, West African talking drums and a thumping beat suggesting South African house music.

Another South African, Sjava, sings fervently in Zulu in "Seasons," a slow soul vamp that makes way for raps from two Californians, Mozzy and Reason, about being trapped in a cycle of institutional racism, poverty and violence.

Those aren't problems that a song or a superhero can solve. But if "Black Panther" had wanted simple comic-book escapism, it wouldn't have hired Mr. Lamar.

# Kendrick Lamar Shakes Up the Pulitzer Game: Let's Discuss

BY JON PARELES AND ZACHARY WOOLFE | APRIL 17, 2018

THE PULITZER PRIZES startled a lot of people this year with an award that's usually greeted as an afterthought: the music prize, which went to Kendrick Lamar's album "DAMN." It was not only the first time a music Pulitzer was given to a hip-hop album, but also to any work outside the more rarefied precincts of classical and, occasionally, jazz composition — indeed, to an album that reached No. 1 on the pop chart. And while it has been reported that "DAMN." was the unanimous choice of the Pulitzer music jury, the award was met in other quarters with disgruntlement and even outrage. Here, Zachary Woolfe, the classical music editor of The New York Times, and Jon Pareles, the chief pop music critic, discuss the choice.

**JON PARELES** To me, this prize is as overdue as it was unexpected. When I look at the Pulitzers across the board, what I overwhelmingly see rewarded are journalistic virtues: fact-gathering, vivid detail, storytelling, topicality, verbal dexterity and, often, real-world impact after publication. It's an award for hard-won persuasiveness. Well hello, hip-hop.

**ZACHARY WOOLFE** One comment I read on Facebook, from a gifted young composer and pianist, was "I have complicated feelings about this, but also, I mean, about damn time." Yes, and yes. There seems to be broad agreement, which I join, about the quality of "DAMN." — its complexity and sensitivity, its seductive confidence and unity, its dense weaving of the personal and political, the religious and sexual.

But there is also wariness, which I join, about an opening of the prize — not to hip-hop, per se, but to music that has achieved blockbuster commercial success. This is now officially one fewer guaranteed platform — which, yes, should be open to many genres —

for noncommercial work, which scrapes by on grants, fellowships, commissions and, yes, awards.

**PARELES** That response is similar to many publishing-world reactions when Bob Dylan got the Nobel Prize in Literature — that a promotional opportunity was being lost for something worthy but more obscure, preferably between hard covers. A literary figure who had changed the way an entire generation looked at words and ideas was supposed to forgo the award because, well, he'd reached too many people? Do we really want to put a sales ceiling on what should get an award? The New York Times and The New Yorker already have a lot of subscribers ... uh-oh.

**WOOLFE** I don't think there is a universal desire for the Nobel to reward obscurity; I'm sure many who were skeptical of Mr. Dylan's win would have been just fine with the best-selling Philip Roth. But it has felt for decades like an integral part of the Pulitzer's mission is to shine a light on corners of music that are otherwise nearly ignored by the broader culture. The award has acted as a reminder — though long a way too stylistically limited one — that artmaking exists beyond the Billboard (and now Spotify) charts.

"DAMN." is surely deserving, yet its victory feels like another sign of the world, and therefore the musical culture, we live in — embodied by the streaming services, through which the biggest artists and albums get more and more, and everyone else gets a smaller piece of the pie. This system is corrosive to music, period — classical, jazz, hip-hop, everything. It's the reality — and there are certainly a lot of very popular artists who are very meaningful, Mr. Lamar among them — but I don't like every aspect of it.

**PARELES** I completely agree with you about the unhealthy overall effects of winner-take-all culture. The word "trending" makes me instinctively recoil; as critics, you and I both want to direct people beyond popularity charts. But choosing "DAMN." wasn't a capitulation

Kendrick Lamar performs in Phoenix, Ariz., on July 12, 2017. The rapper is the first Pulitzer Prize for Music winner who is not a classical or jazz musician.

to mere popularity. The album is a complex, varied, subtle, richly multilayered work, overflowing with ideas and by no means immediately ingratiating. You have to give it genuine attention and thought to get the most out of it, just as with any other Pulitzer-winning composition.

Meanwhile, wasn't the music Pulitzer, for many decades, largely the captive of a small, insular academic music scene? The Pulitzers refused a special citation for Duke Ellington, who never won the award. They ignored jazz — artistically subtle and sublime, commercially endangered — until Wynton Marsalis finally got a Pulitzer in 1997. They were unconscionably late — looking awfully cliquish to me — even in recognizing Minimalism: Steve Reich got his Pulitzer in 2009, not in 1977 for "Music for 18 Musicians."

To me, it looks like some of the squawks are complaints about exclusivity being breached. And if you ask me, it should have happened sooner. I hereby nominate, for a retrospective Pulitzer, Public Enemy's 1988 album "It Takes a Nation of Millions to Hold Us Back": an experimental sonic bombshell, a verbal torrent, a mind expander. For that matter, the Pulitzers were late on Kendrick Lamar, too: "To Pimp a Butterfly," from 2015, has even more musical breadth than "DAMN." (which has plenty).

**WOOLFE** There have been so many missed opportunities. The year after it turned down Ellington — the main Pulitzer board rejected the music jury's recommendation — it could have given the regular prize to Coltrane's "A Love Supreme." How about Joni Mitchell's "Blue," which could have won in 1972 — she's Canadian and therefore ineligible, but remember, this is my fantasy world — over a decade before the prize finally got around to recognizing a female composer? Philip Glass, never quite beloved in the academic realm, remains Pulitzer-less. And I'll just leave this right here: Kanye.

You could play these games forever. It is belated and necessary that the award widen to encompass a fuller picture of what music is. But if that widening further marginalizes noncommercial work — which doesn't view itself as exclusive but simply as endangered in an economic system that conspires against it — something important will be lost. Responsible eclecticism is what I'd want going forward from Pulitzer juries, for whom the "DAMN." award will hopefully be freeing in the best sense.

**PARELES** What were the pieces from the other two finalists, Ted Hearne and Michael Gilbertson?

**WOOLFE** Like Mr. Lamar, who's 30, these guys are strikingly young. Mr. Gilbertson, 30 as well, wrote a string quartet that veers from glassy to robust, and Mr. Hearne, 35, wrote "Sound From the Bench," a cantata for chamber choir, electric guitars and drums. Like Mr. Lamar's album, the finalists are politically charged: Mr. Hearne, always socially conscious, here mashes up texts from Supreme Court decisions to suggest the ambiguities of identity and humanity. (A corporation has speech, you say?) And Mr. Gilbertson has said that he adjusted his initial sketches for his quartet after the 2016 election, making them "more introspective and comforting." Almost as significant as Mr. Lamar's win, for me, is the trio taken together: a new generation, turning the world around it into music.

**PARELES** I'll have to put them in a playlist. I'm not suggesting that the Pulitzers mirror the Top 10 or the Grammys. (Please, no.) And next year, sure, give the prize to an album that sold 11 copies after a lone college gig somewhere. But I think we're seeing a shifting perspective on the way contemporary classical and jazz composition often draw on the ideas of hip-hop or world music or pop, as if to elevate them by carrying them into the concert hall.

According to the Pulitzer reporting, "DAMN." got added to consideration when the jury was looking into a composition with hip-hop influences, and decided to go to the source — where the ideas, in this case, are even stronger, both rawer and smarter. The prize citation praises "DAMN." for its "vernacular authenticity and rhythmic dynamism," which to me has a whiff of condescension — there's all sorts of brainpower and artifice in there, too — but let's enjoy the win. Regarding noncommercial outreach, Mr. Lamar often collaborates with first-rate, innovative jazz musicians, like Kamasi Washington, who not only are happy to work with him but also benefit — in their own audience growth — from showing up in his album credits.

One thing that also strikes me about giving the award to "DAMN." is that it quietly sets aside two previous Pulitzer givens: that the winning piece was performed by live musicians in real time and that it was written by a solitary composer. But "DAMN." has multiple producers, composers and performers (even Rihanna and U2 cameos!) layering tracks in studios. Mr. Lamar is the auteur, fully in charge but not the sole creator. It's another way of making music that deserves respect.

**WOOLFE** This year's Pulitzer actually reinforced that old Romantic illusion of the singular composer. It was given to Mr. Lamar alone — not, as in the Grammys, to the album's songwriting or producing teams, too.

**PARELES** Maybe they should change the citation to "Kendrick Lamar and staff" — like the reporting prizes. To me, both the Dylan Nobel and the Lamar Pulitzer — which is not the first hip-hop Pulitzer; Lin-Manuel Miranda got that for drama with "Hamilton" — are signals that the old prize-giving institutions are rethinking the ways in which they used to circumscribe the idea of quality. As long as they're conscientious, that can make the awards only more significant.

# CHAPTER 4

# Drake

Aubrey Drake Graham, better known by the stage name Drake, has changed the face of hip-hop with his distinctive musical styling and confessional lyrics. Drake was raised in Canada, where he had early success playing a character on the teenage television show "Degrassi." Since he turned to rap in 2007, Drake has consistently broken musical records, becoming one of the most celebrated and best-selling musicians in the world. The articles in this chapter reflect his critical and commercial success.

# The New Face of Hip-Hop

BY JON CARAMANICA | JUNE 9, 2010

LOS ANGELES — In March the young hip-hop star Drake was in town for a harried few days, polishing up the final details on his debut album, "Thank Me Later," and filming the video for the first single, "Over," before heading out on his first proper headlining tour. On his last night, his team was holed up at the studio in the basement of the Sunset Marquis hotel, accessible only by special elevator.

Earlier in the day Jay-Z had sent him an encouraging e-mail message that paraphrased one of his own lyrics: "Things are going good/ But good can turn to better." Taking a break to eat before settling in for an all-night session at the studio, Drake checked his phone and laughed. He was texting with someone he was pretty certain was Halle Berry; LeBron James, a close friend, thought he'd be a great match for Ms. Berry's cousin, and Ms. Berry seemed to be feeling him out.

For most of his teenage years Drake, tall, broad and handsome, was still known as Aubrey Graham (Drake is his middle name) and played the basketball star Jimmy Brooks on the popular Canadian teenage drama "Degrassi: The Next Generation." In the last 18 months, though, he's become the most important and innovative new figure in hip-hop, and an unlikely one at that. Biracial Jewish-Canadian former child actors don't have a track record of success in the American rap industry.

But when "Thank Me Later" (Aspire/Young Money/Cash Money) is released this week, it will cement Drake's place among hip-hop's elite. It's a moody, entrancing and emotionally articulate album that shows off Drake's depth as a rapper, a singer and a songwriter, without sacrificing accessibility. That he does all those things well marks him as an adept student of the last 15 years: there's Jay-Z's attention to detail, Kanye West's gift for melody, Lil Wayne's street-wise pop savvy.

In rapid fashion Drake has become part of hip-hop's DNA, leapfrogging any number of more established rappers. "I'm where I truly deserve to be," Drake said over quesadillas at the hotel's lobby bar. "I believe in myself, in my presence, enough that I don't feel small in Jay's presence. I don't feel small in Wayne's presence."

But "Thank Me Later" is fluent enough in hip-hop's traditions deftly to abandon them altogether in places. Finally his outsider background has become an asset. As a rapper, Drake manages to balance vulnerability and arrogance in equal measure, a rare feat. He also sings — not with technological assistance, as other rappers do, but expertly.

Then there's his subject matter: not violence or drugs or streetcorner bravado. Instead emotions are what fuel Drake, 23, who has an almost pathological gift for connection. Great eye contact. Easy smile. Evident intelligence. Quick to ask questions. "He's a kid that can really work the room, whatever the room," said his mother, Sandi Graham. "Thank Me Later" has its share of bluster, but is more notable for its regret, its ache.

Drake performing at S.O.B.'s in New York in May 2009.

As for Ms. Berry's cousin, Drake's interested, of course, but wary. "I think I have to live this life for a little bit longer before I even know what love is in this atmosphere," he said. More fame only means less feeling, he knows.

Dodging vulnerability has been a fact of Drake's life since childhood. His parents split when he was 3. An only child, he lived with his mother, who soon began battling rheumatoid arthritis, a condition that eventually prevented her from working, forcing Drake to become responsible at a young age. "We would have this little drill where, Lord forbid something happened, if there was a fire or an emergency, he would have to run outside and get a neighbor and call 911," Ms. Graham said. His father, Dennis, who is black, was an intermittent presence — sometimes struggling with drugs, sometimes in jail.

"One thing I wasn't was sheltered from the pains of adulthood," Drake said. When something upset him as a teenager, he often told himself: "That's just the right now. I can change that. I can change anything. The hand that was dealt doesn't exist to me.' "

From an early age he'd been interested in performing, whether rewriting the lyrics to "Mary Had a Little Lamb" or spending time as a child model. By then, he and his mother were living in Forest Hill, a well-to-do, heavily Jewish neighborhood on the north side of Toronto, where he attended local schools, often the only black student in sight. His mother is white and Jewish, and Drake had a bar mitzvah. At school he struggled academically and socially. "Character-building moments, but not great memories," he recalled. In eighth grade he got an agent and was soon sent off to audition for "Degrassi: The Next Generation," an updated version of the popular 1980s Canadian drama.

He auditioned after school, on the same day, he said, that he first smoked pot from a bong. Nevertheless he landed the role of the wealthy, well-liked basketball star Jimmy Brooks, who was originally conceived as a white football player.

"Part of his journey is trying to figure where he does fit in in the world, having a white Jewish mom and a black, often absentee father," said Linda Schuyler, a creator of the show. "It's almost a comfort factor with Jimmy Brooks. That was the antithesis of his life at the time. It was probably reassuring and a bit escapist for him to play that role."

Sometimes he was hiding even when the cameras were off, sleeping on the show's set. "When I woke up in the morning, I was still the guy that could act and laugh," he said. "It's just that home was overwhelming." Along with "Degrassi" came a new, more diverse school closer to the set, where he first tried rapping in public. As he got older, he also tried out his verses on one of his father's jailhouse friends, who listened over the phone.

In 2006 Drake, then an acolyte of hip-hop's thoughtful bohemian wing, released his first mixtape, "Room for Improvement." He also was testing out the rapper lifestyle, spending money — some from "Degrassi," some borrowed from family and friends — out of step with his actual earning.

He leased a Rolls-Royce Phantom, parking it on the street outside the family's apartment, much to his mother's chagrin. "Who drives a Phantom and doesn't have a place to park it?" Ms. Graham remembers asking her son. "And what's even more embarrassing is we owe so much money and we have so many debts and bills."

Summers were spent with his father's side of the family, in Memphis, where one of his cousins was dating the manager of the rapper Yo Gotti. There Drake gained an affection for the energy of Southern rap, which contrasted with the headier material he had started out making himself.

The New Orleans rap star Lil Wayne heard Drake's music in the summer of 2008 and invited him out on the road. "I sat in the same place on the bus for a week," Drake recalled. "I was scared." Wayne only found out about Drake's acting past when he landed on "Degrassi" while flipping channels on the bus's television.

In short order Drake became a key part of Wayne's touring madhouse, and whenever there was downtime, in a studio or hotel room, he worked on songs. The outcome was "So Far Gone," his third mixtape and one of last year's best-received hip-hop recordings. It's one of the most ambivalent, melancholy documents of rap success ever released, which is odd, because it was recorded long before Drake's turn in the limelight.

On "So Far Gone" he sought to cultivate multiple audiences at once: in addition to straight-ahead rap songs, he also rapped over instrumentals from indie acts like Santigold, Lykke Li and Peter Bjorn & John. "That was supposed to be the wild and crazy project we did to get that out of our system before we put out a really generic rap album," said Oliver el-Khatib, Drake's longtime friend and de facto creative consultant.

Most notably, he sang — some songs in their entirety. In part that was a response to heartbreak: he'd been trying to shake loose of a destructive relationship with a manipulative woman who had taunted him with the fact that she had previously been involved with a famous rap star. The wounded R&B songs are about her. "I don't even know if I wrote a rap song in that whole nine months," Drake said, "because

I wasn't a rapper anymore. I didn't believe in myself. I was someone else's property." (He was so uncertain about the sung tracks on "So Far Gone" that he tried to get them placed on an album by his friend the R&B singer Trey Songz — fortunately, with no luck.)

His next relationship was better: it inspired "Best I Ever Had," the bawdy song that became his breakthrough solo hit. It reached No. 2 on the Billboard Hot 100, practically unheard of for a song that originated on a mixtape. Eventually it would earn Drake a pair of 2010 Grammy nominations, a first for a rapper with no album out. (An abridged EP version was eventually released to stores to capitalize on Drake's raised mainstream profile. It has sold almost 500,000 copies, a surprising number for a collection of songs widely available free online.)

An endorsement deal with Sprite (which led to a bizarro commercial in which Drake's body splits into pieces, then reforms) was already being negotiated before Drake's record deal was complete. "The fact that he has a background that differs from your prototypical rap artist — from Toronto, multiracial, the fact that he was a child actor — corporate America, they're attracted to that," said Shawn Gee, Drake's business manager.

But Drake's difference has also made him a target. In May 2009 he was robbed at gunpoint in a Toronto restaurant. He cooperated with the police investigation, in what some perceived as a violation of hip-hop's no-snitching ethos. The black gossip Web site MediaTakeout.com posted a snapshot of a page of the criminal complaint under the headline "Caught Snitchin!!! Rapper Drake Testifying Against Men Who Robbed Him!!!"

"I feel unsafe in Toronto at all times," Drake said. "I'm a one of one. There's no one else you can hate as much as me if you hate money, or you hate success." Reminders of fame's dark side are all around him. Since March his mentor and label boss, Lil Wayne, has been on Rikers Island serving a one-year sentence in connection with a 2007 gun charge. This month Drake visited him there for the first time. "That's not the place for him," Drake said.

"A lot of 'So Far Gone' was predictions," he said. "I was rapping about things I'm only going through now." As a result "Thank Me Later" often feels like a memoir: Drake is the rare pop artist who seems to think of himself in the past tense. On "Light Up" he raps, "I keep thinking, 'How young could you die from old age?' "

For a first single, "Over" was particularly paranoid and cheerless. "I know way too many people here right now/That I didn't know last year," he sings at the chorus. As if to prove the point, at the video shoot just outside Los Angeles, which was meant to be private, the hangar-size studio filled up with hangers-on over the course of the long night, including the actor Ryan Phillippe, a friend of the director. "Thank you for coming," Drake said, his face a blend of gratitude and bewilderment.

On "The Resistance" he raps about an accidental pregnancy with a woman he was briefly involved with, who chose to end the pregnancy. And on "Fireworks" there's a verse about Rihanna, who asked him last year to write a song for her new album; the two soon began seeing each other regularly, though they never publicly confirmed their brief relationship.

"I was a pawn," Drake said. The song he wrote for her never got released. "You know what she was doing to me? She was doing exactly what I've done to so many women throughout my life, which is show them quality time, then disappear," he said. "I was like, wow, this feels terrible."

But it's also the new normal, and Drake wonders if real intimacy is now out of reach, maybe irretrievably so. "Did I sacrifice something?" he asked, looking for the black cloud above the silver lining. "Have I not realized what it is yet because I'm enjoying this too much?"

# Drake: Rapper, Actor, Meme

BY JON CARAMANICA | OCT. 23, 2015

IN THE BEGINNING, Drake's "Hotline Bling" was a pure child of the Internet. Released in July on his label's SoundCloud page following a premiere on Apple Music's OVO Sound Radio, it felt like a casual throwaway, a breezy compatriot to "Charged Up," his anti-Meek Mill song, which landed at the same time.

And yet "Hotline Bling," a song about romantic disappointment and shortcomings, which moves at a slow shuffle, has become a surprise radio hit and is currently at No. 2 in the country.

This week, though, the Internet decided it wanted "Hotline Bling" back. Late Monday night, Drake released its video, mostly made up of long shots of him dancing in front of a plain background that's constantly changing colors: mustard, lavender, baby blue, peach, chartreuse. The clip, directed by Director X, is both warm and slick, giving this song — part of the lo-fi catharsis segment of Drake's catalog — the grand-scale sensation that thoughtfully minimalist approaches can trigger.

The "Hotline Bling" video is also the moment when Drake fully becomes a meme.

No celebrity understands the mechanisms of Internet obsession better than Drake. Online, fandom isn't merely an act of receiving — it's one of interaction, recontextualization, disputed ownership and cheek. For the celebrity, it's about letting go of unilateral top-down narratives and letting the hive take control. For fans, it's about applying personalization to the object of adoration.

The "Hotline Bling" video is built exactly for that task. It's important at its full length, but even more so in the screenshots and few-seconds-long GIFs that it's designed to be broken down into. It's less a video than an open source code that easily allows Drake's image and gestures to be rewritten, drawn over, repurposed.

In part, that has to do with the unclutteredness of the video, which mostly surrounds Drake with blank space. There's also the nature of the dancing itself, which is also more or less blank: a series of slight shifts of weight, quick hand gestures, head bobbles and side-to-side steps. They're small moves that he repeats — in essence, he's making a GIF of himself, anticipating what will inevitably happen to him online.

There's also nothing contemporary about the moves — no dabbing, no whip, no hitting the quan. Instead, they're concise, universal, more about implication than full expression. They're also relatable and a little bit goofy, another mechanism of approachability.

Because of that, they can be mapped onto almost anything, which is exactly what the Internet did. Within hours — minutes, really — Twitter and Vine and Instagram and Tumblr were filled with short clips pulled from the video set to other songs: Elvis Crespo's merengue conflagration "Suavemente," the "Seinfeld" theme, "Danza Kuduro," various Vince Guaraldi ditties from "Peanuts," and, most crucially, "Obsesion" by the bachata boy band Aventura. (If there is a style parent to Drake's dance micro-moves, it is probably bachata.) Often these clips were accompanied by the hashtag #DrakeAlwaysOnBeat, though, strictly speaking, he wasn't.

The most ambitious memes, however, did more than marry the video to new audio; they tweaked the video. One took a segment where Drake was swatting his arm and put a tennis racket in his hand, making him thwack away balls fired at him. Another replaced the music with the zippy horns of the later-seasons theme song from "The Cosby Show," overlaying the video with a credits scroll for "The Aubrey Show." (Drake's given name is Aubrey Drake Graham.) Most technically impressive was the clip that superimposed lightsabers into the hands of Drake and his dance partner-choreographer, Tanisha Scott.

Drake, of course, knew all of this would happen. "We were looking at playbacks, and he was like, 'This is totally going to be a meme,' " Ms. Scott told Complex.

Transparency has always been Drake's bailiwick, but this approach to content creation takes it past a place of emotional vulnerability and into an advanced space where an artist induces people to create their own narratives: The star is at the center, but not in control. Making a meme of a celebrity can be a way to sort through complex feelings of fandom. It's an act of devotion, and also undermining. Drake, more than anyone, understands that this will happen whether or not he wants, so why should everyone else have all the fun? He wants to play, too.

This moment of full meme absorption comes just as Drake and the art world have been dancing around — and sometimes with — each other. Last year, he took a writer for Rolling Stone to the Los Angeles County Museum of Art to see an exhibition by James Turrell, whose influence is strong on the "Hotline Bling" video. This summer, he partnered with Sotheby's to help promote a gallery show of contemporary black art.

Art has been on Drake's mind since at least 2011, when, on the song "Dreams Money Can Buy," he rapped, "I got car money, fresh start money/I want Saudi money, I want art money." Like many rappers faced with growing wealth and outmoded options for what to do with it, he understands art as a different layer of class transcendence — something beyond expensive clothes, cars, houses. (In this, he follows rappers like Jay Z, collector of Basquiat and imitator of Marina Abramovic; Kanye West, who has collaborated with Takashi Murakami, Vanessa Beecroft, George Condo; and Swizz Beatz, a well-regarded collector and sometime artist.)

Drake is something of a meme artist himself, or at minimum a meme archivist-historian. That was clear in August at his OVO Fest in Toronto, where he definitively ended his squabble with Meek Mill by displaying a slide show of savage memes pulled from the Internet behind him as he performed "Charged Up" and his other Meek Mill attack, "Back to Back."

He also recently appeared on the cover of W magazine's art issue, where part of the feature involved five artists — Kaws, Jim Joe, Mark Flood, Henry Taylor, Katherine Bernhardt — offering artistic interpretations of Drake.

This is a clever solution to an old problem: how to differentiate one celebrity magazine cover from all the others. But it's also consistent with the appropriative license many artists online have been taking with Drake's image for years now. Thanks to Tumblr and Instagram and a generation raised on the cut-and-paste values of the Internet, Drake art has been ubiquitous online for some time. Mostly, it lives at the intersection of high art and fan art — high fan art?

A year ago, the Brooklyn artists Grace Miceli and Shana Sadeghi-Ray curated a collection of Drake-themed projects on the website Art Baby Gallery. Over the summer, Ms. Miceli — who makes a T-shirt representing Drake lyrics in the style of Jenny Holzer's "Inflammatory Essays" — curated a group show at Alt Space that included a handful of Drake-related pieces. And on Saturday — Drake's 29th birthday, as it happens — Living Gallery in Brooklyn will host a Drake-themed party and art show featuring the work of five artists, including Daren Chambers, whose work as True Minimalist is popular on Instagram.

"Hotline Bling" isn't the first time Drake has become clip art for social media. Memorably, in 2013, a photo taken of him on the set of DJ Khaled's "No New Friends" video, which caught him mid-pose wearing a throwback Damani Dada athletic outfit, became a web sensation. One company even began manufacturing polo shirts with the picture embroidered on the chest.

Of course, what did Drake do when he found out about those shirts? He ordered some. What did he do with the video of him dancing to Aventura? He posted it to his own Instagram account. And True Minimalist's sketches? They're there, too, along with all sorts of Drake fan art. You don't meme Drake; Drake memes Drake.

That tail-swallowing has accelerated to the point where the original content almost begins to blur. And yet not, because all of these videos — the Vines, the Instagram shorts, the YouTube clips — they all spanned the song's reach. Drake got "Hotline Bling" to No. 2; maybe the Internet can get it to No 1.

# On 'Views,' Drake
# Is Still His Own Genre

REVIEW | BY JON CARAMANICA | APRIL 29, 2016

DRAKE'S CAREER HAS been built on collapsing walls, and "One Dance," one of the early singles from his new album, "Views," is a vivacious fulfillment of his promise as hip-hop's great syncretic hope.

Rapped and sung, sprinkled with patois, made in collaboration with the Nigerian Afrobeats star Wizkid and sampling Kyla's "Do You Mind" (a smash on Britain's funky dance music scene in the late 2000s), "One Dance" is a transnational dance-floor lullaby, one of Drake's breeziest and most accessible songs, and also one of his savviest.

But "One Dance," gentle as it is, is also about fear. "Streets not safe/but I never run away," he sings, in a dulcet voice.

"I pray to make it back in one piece/I pray, I pray/that's why I need one dance," he continues, connecting his urge to live with his urge to move.

It is perhaps the purest distillation of the current state of Drake: globally ambitious, ruthlessly effective, skeptical and wary. A pop star with rap star anxieties. An emperor wondering about the state of his clothes.

"Views" — Drake's fourth solo album, not counting umpteen mixtapes and other ephemera — finds him a conqueror between territories: fending off attacks from below, maintaining his grip on turf he controls and wondering what might be next.

Crucially, it's not the acidic Drake that's taken center stage in the last year and a half, on the mixtape "If You're Reading This It's Too Late" and his collaborative album with Future, "What a Time to Be Alive." Those releases showed Drake at his most indignant, a left-field turn from the emotionally lavish music he'd built his reputation on.

"Views" shows how Drake's original sound has become a genre unto itself — not just as a template for others but also for Drake himself. The framework pioneered by him and his right-hand producer, 40 — tender, lush, soothing melodies about romantic vulnerability — can be used for songs about heartbreak, but also for songs about competitive stress, mistrust and fear.

Not that he's abandoned one-sided relationship talks. The most vivid one here is the fretful and class-concerned "Childs Play":

*You wildin', you super childish, you go to CVS for*
*Kotex in my Bugatti, I took the key and tried to*
*hide it so you can't drive it, and put on mileage*
*Then you find it, awkward silence*

On "U With Me?," which recalls his excellent "Paris Morton Music 2," Drake looks for love on his phone: "I group DM my exes/I tell 'em they belong to me, that goes on for forever"; "three dots, you thinking of a reaction still."

But love is, increasingly, about money, too. "Sell my secrets and get top dollar/Sell my secrets for a Range Rover," he says on "Redemption," then continues: "Who's gonna save me when I need saving?/ Since 'Take Care,' I've been caretaking."

Drake is more preoccupied with cadence than most rappers, and of course, more able to make unexpected juxtapositions between rapping and singing than anyone else. And thanks to his flirtations with dancehall, Afrobeats and grime, he is as flexible as ever. That's why the most exciting moments on "Views" may be structural: Drake rapping in gnawed-off chunks like 2 Chainz on "Hype," or with streamlined Jamaican inflections on "Controlla," or with the dead-eyed stomp of Chicago drill music on "Pop Style."

"Views" is dauntingly long, and Drake still hears his inner narrative as biblical epic — take the album's opener, "Keep the Family Close," where he sings with resignation and pomp, "All of my let's-just-be-friends are friends I don't have anymore/How do you not check on me when things go wrong?" He typically ends his albums with what could be termed a talk track, an extended rumination on the state of his feelings. On "Views," there are several such songs sprinkled throughout the album.

But there are risks to effectively becoming your own genre — understudies and comers will do what they can to follow what you've already done, but so will you. Overall, "Views" contains Drake's most straightforward lyrics, and his emotional excavations aren't as striking as they were a few years ago, when they had the sting of the new to them.

Drake is becoming more walled off as a person, too. He uses social media brilliantly, but not revealingly. He has largely forsworn the news media. Last year, reference demo tracks for a handful of his songs recorded by Quentin Miller, a frequent collaborator, leaked online, suggesting Drake may not have written his own songs, but Drake barely addressed the controversy. When the rapper Meek Mill publicly accused Drake of false advertising, Drake replied with great songs, not an outburst.

Given the intensity of that controversy, it's notable that, as of this writing, Drake hasn't released the songwriting credits for "Views." There was even a transparency hiccup during the album's release. Drake's producer 40 posted a list of the album producers on his Instagram, then posted an update including names of producers he overlooked in the first post.

The only public interview Drake has done for "Views" came Thursday night, when he sat for a brief chat with the Beats 1 radio host Zane Lowe. Despite the controlled setting — an employee of Apple Music speaking with one of the company's biggest celebrity partners — there was honesty that couldn't help but peek through: the way Drake began swallowing words when tiptoeing around why the original version of "Pop Style" that included Kanye West and Jay Z didn't make the album, or his gritted-teeth replies when discussing his occasionally frosty history with the Weeknd, a onetime collaborator.

Most vivid, though, there was the heavy muscle and heavier patois he employed when talking about younger Toronto artists following in his footsteps while taking shots at him — "coming for the don," he called it. If Drake was betraying even a hint of vulnerability or frustration on those other topics, here he was bulked up and on message.

For the last seven years, Drake has recentered hip-hop around melody and feeling; turned his hometown, Toronto, into an aesthetic hotbed; and become one of pop music's most transformational, and doubted, figures. But all that has come with a price: the realization that the only way to protect your heart is with armor.

# On Drake's 'More Life,' the Creator Meets the Curator

REVIEW | BY JON CARAMANICA | MARCH 20, 2017

FOR ALMOST A DECADE, Drake has been a star and also a curator, the artist most responsible for hip-hop's evolutionary changes and the one most likely to spot the next in line for the crown.

He has also been a bit of a formal innovator — he releases albums, and also mixtapes, as well as loosies when the feeling strikes. The traditional album cycle may be on the verge of extinction in the pop sphere; Drake has made peace with that.

His latest project, "More Life" — which had its premiere Saturday on OVO Sound Radio, his label's weekly show on Apple Music's Beats 1 radio station, and is available on all major platforms for streaming and sale — is billed not as an album, or a mixtape, but a playlist, a choice that has both rhetorical and business import.

Since Billboard tweaked its rules to include streaming, playlists are eligible to appear on the album chart, something that a handful of record labels have taken advantage of with compilations, but no major stand-alone artist has taken on as a creative challenge — Drake is the first. Having a blockbuster success with something other than a traditional album would encourage other artists to experiment with format. And codifying the playlist as a delivery mechanism for new music, not just for collecting other people's songs, is a conceptual boon for streaming services, including Apple Music, with which Drake has had a longtime partnership.

But the playlist also suggests an aesthetic shift from the album, which in its platonic ideal form is narratively structured and contained, a creator's complete thought expressed in parts. A playlist in the streaming era, by contrast, is a collection of moods, impressions, influences and references; it's a river that flows in one direction, ending somewhere far from the beginning (if it ends at all).

Drake performing in July in Austin, Tex. His latest project, "More Life," debuted on Saturday on OVO Sound Radio, his label's show on Apple Music's Beats 1 radio station.

This format — relaxed, circuitous, able to take in both his own work and also work by others — is particularly well suited to Drake, who's as definable by his taste as by his sound.

And so goes the often captivating "More Life," a nuanced collection of 22 new songs that recall various stages of Drake's own development, as well as a tour of other styles and artists that he's partial to. It is both craven and elegant — a collection that's well matched to the medium and a logical extension of what Drake has been offering for years.

He doesn't overdeliver on the concept: "More Life" is the length of a very long album, not long enough to accompany a marathon. Where it differs from a Drake album is in how he comports himself and imports others. "More Life" takes a whole host of voices seriously — not just Drake's but also guests who are given plenty of room.

"4422" is a full song from the aching soul man Sampha; "Skepta Interlude" is a more or less full brute-strength song from the British grime rapper Skepta; "Glow," a duet with Kanye West, leans heavily in Mr. West's direction. The tough grime veteran Giggs appears on two songs, shining with a hilariously lewd verse on "KMT." Young Thug also shows up twice, delivering mystical singing on "Sacrifices" and showing why he's the clearest modern-day inheritor of P-Funk on "Ice Melts."

This is a lot of competing energy, and on a traditional album, it might all have to serve a common purpose. But "More Life" is exciting for its detours, its crevices, its relaxed saunter across the various lanes of forward-thinking hip-hop and soul.

Drake is here, too, of course — saving his best rapping for a more formal project, perhaps, but still wound up about being let down by women and also by men. Drake is still in the paranoid and resentful mode that has dominated the last three years, but even when he's lashing out, he feels gentler and more resigned. "People like you more when you working towards something/Not when you have it," he raps on "Lose You." Again and again, his fatigue is a theme, as on "Jorja Interlude": "Told me I'm looking exhausted/You hit it right on the nose." At the end of "Can't Have Everything," Drake's mother shows up in what appears to be a voice mail message, cautioning her son against confrontation and anxiety.

Drake loves to hear people talk, both for what they say and how they say it. A scholar of accents and attitude, he lets other people set the mood on "More Life" in several places with sampled spoken interludes. They're intimate breaks deployed by an artist who's often said he's seeking to provide a soundtrack for his listeners' lives, to get in their heads. (Drake is, almost without question, the single greatest source of perfectly pitched Instagram captions.)

Mouth-to-ear transaction is the level Drake excels at. Consider what Drake doesn't do: He's the biggest pop star not named Beyoncé who doesn't traffic in the trite big-tent on-the-one dance music that's chart-dominant and soul-killing. He doesn't make songs for getting lost in a crowd; he makes songs for getting lost in your feelings.

Not that he eschews the dance floor. Instead of aiming for dull festival grandeur, he emphasizes the movement's black roots — he's partial to house music (as heard here on the sensual "Passionfruit"), dancehall, Nigerian Afrobeats. His range is as musically meaningful as the one demonstrated by Beyoncé on "Lemonade" — her investigation was intranational, delving into country and slashing rock; Drake's is international and diasporic, with a keen ear for how the internet has brought even closer black music from North America, the Caribbean, Europe and Africa.

Increasingly, Drake is as much ethnomusicologist as outright collaborator, a shift from the days when he would wield his influence by helping shepherd artists like Migos and Future out of regional acclaim into something wider by appearing on a remix. But even at this more advanced level, he is still scavenging for the latest sound, as heard on "KMT," where he borrows the jaunty staccato pattern found in the current viral hit "Look at Me" by XXXTentacion. Drake is a teacher to many, but he's still a hungry student, too.

# Drake's 'Scorpion' Is a Streaming Giant

BY BEN SISARIO | JULY 2, 2018

IF THERE WAS any doubt before, it is now official: Drake is the king of streaming music.

When his 25-track new album, "Scorpion," was released on Friday, it immediately shattered one-day streaming records at the major services. In its first 24 hours, the album had 170 million streams on Apple Music around the world. On Spotify, where at one point the album was being listened to 10 million times an hour, it logged at least 132 million streams globally, according to unofficial tallies. (Spotify declined to provide specific numbers.) Through Sunday, "Scorpion" had a total of 435 million streams, according to Billboard. That beat the previous weekly streaming record, held by Post Malone with 431 million, in just three days.

The promotion for "Scorpion" shows just how intensely the streaming services will compete for the clicks of a major event record. Apple, which has had a close association with Drake for years, put Siri to work with a list of his nicknames. Spotify made Drake the face of dozens of playlists — even some that contained no Drake songs. His full coronation on the Billboard chart will not come until next week, when his totals are computed.

On Billboard's current chart, the No. 1 album is Panic! at the Disco's "Pray for the Wicked," which had 38 million streams and sold 151,000 copies as a full album, giving it an equivalent of 180,000 sales for the week.

In the wake of the rapper XXXTentacion's death, his album "?" continued to dominate streaming services (at least until "Scorpion" came around), and he had two albums in the Top 5: "?" moved up one spot to No. 2, and "17" moved up two spots to No. 5. XXXTentacion's song "Sad!," which had jumped to No. 1 on the Hot 100 singles chart, fell to No. 2; Cardi B's "I Like It," featuring Bad Bunny and J Balvin, moved in to the top spot.

Drake performs in Austin, Tex., July 20, 2016.

Also on this week's album chart, Post Malone's "Beerbongs & Bentleys" is No. 3, and "Everything Is Love," the joint album by the Carters (a.k.a. Beyoncé and Jay-Z), is No. 4.

Last week's top seller, 5 Seconds of Summer's "Youngblood," fell to No. 10.

# CHAPTER 5

# Cardi B

Belcalis Marlenis Almanzar, known professionally as Cardi B, took an unusual route to hip-hop fame: She developed her following on Instagram, where she posted videos documenting her life as a stripper. This landed her a role on VH1's "Love & Hip Hop." When she released her single "Bodak Yellow" in 2017, it became the undisputed song of the summer. The articles in this chapter show Cardi B's rise to success and how she has managed life as a rap star.

## An Afternoon With Cardi B as She Makes Money Moves

BY JOANNA NIKAS  |  AUG. 17, 2017

BELCALIS ALMANZAR, known as Cardi B to her growing number of fans, stepped into the W hotel in Midtown Manhattan wearing leggings, an Atlanta Braves "Los Bravos" logo jersey and white Yeezy sneakers. She breezed past a bellhop, who was rapping her hit song, "Bodak Yellow (Money Moves)."

This "regular degular schmegular girl from the Bronx," formerly a stripper, built her career on her ability to rattle off one-liners like "I'mma get that schmoney" on the VH1 reality series "Love & Hip Hop." During her time on the show, some viewers saw her as a hero of female empowerment, as she made pronouncements like "Ever since I started using guys, I feel so much better about myself. I feel so damn powerful."

Cardi B on the balcony of her suite at the W hotel in Midtown Manhattan before her Aug. 12 performance at MoMA PS1 in Queens.

Saturday was a big day for the 24-year-old hip-hop star. She had come to the hotel from a sound check at MoMA PS1, in Queens, where she would take the stage that evening.

After releasing two mixtapes, Cardi B signed a deal with Atlantic Records earlier this year. "Bodak Yellow," which is No. 8 on the Billboard Hot 100, has been the rap anthem of the summer, and tonight she would be performing it for the first time at an event open to the public in her hometown.

In the elevator she asked her publicist Patientce Foster, "What are we going to do to celebrate if I'm No. 1?"

"Don't say 'if,' " Ms. Foster said. "When."

"When," Cardi B said.

"Are you going to get a butler named Carlton?" Ms. Foster asked, laughing.

After the elevator reached the 18th floor, Ms. Foster opened the door to a suite with a balcony. Inside was an open suitcase containing three pairs of high-heeled Christian Louboutins with red soles. Cardi B said Louboutins represent wealth, and she refers to them in "Bodak Yellow" as "red bottoms."

She said she got her first pair for her 19th birthday from an admirer at a strip club where she worked. At the time she was amazed at the $800 price tag. The most she had paid for shoes was the $300 she had spent on a pair of Jeffrey Campbells.

Cardi B announced that she was going to take a nap, slipped off her Yeezys and made her way to the bedroom.

Lately she had been going nonstop. She had just come from recording new tracks in Atlanta, the home city of Offset (of the rap group Migos), whom she described as "this boy I'm dating." Before that she was in Toronto, where Drake conferred his blessing by bringing her on stage at the OVO Fest.

Not a half-hour of nap time had passed before Ms. Foster called from the living room: "Bells? I need to start taking out your hair!"

Showtime was 6:45 p.m., and Cardi B needed to have her hair and makeup done.

She took a seat in the living room. Shawnta Loran, who was the makeup artist for Cardi B (back when her stage name was Camilla) and other dancers at Sue's, a strip club in Mount Vernon, N.Y., added some powder to her face with a brush.

"She knew me when I was a roach," Cardi B said of Ms. Loran.

The rapper's use of "roach" made news recently: Some Twitter users had dug up an old Cardi B tweet in which the word appeared, and accused her of using it as a slur against black women with darker skin. Cardi B defended herself, saying it was a common term in the Bronx, with no racist connotations.

She took out her phone and called her father to discuss a car she was about to buy: an orange Bentley Bentayga S.U.V. with "peanut butter" interior, as she described it.

"To drive around Manhattan?" asked another member of her entourage, Marsha St. Hubert, a senior vice president of urban marketing at Atlantic Records. "To drive around *Manhattan*?"

"I am a rapper," Cardi B said. "I need this car."

Ms. Foster pointed out that she didn't have a driver's license.

"I don't know how to drive," Cardi B admitted.

At 6 p.m. her stylist, Kollin Carter, along with his assistant, helped her into a custom LaQuan Smith lace red dress. When she slipped on the Louboutins, she was ready to go.

She rode in the back of a black S.U.V. toward MoMA PS1 with Ashley Kalmanowitz, senior director of publicity at Atlantic Records, Ms. Foster; her 4-year old son, Brave; and Ms. Foster's mother, Pamela Foster. Cardi B entered through the back and immediately found herself in a narrow hallway crowded with people trying to catch a glimpse of her. She had a hard time making her way through the crush of fans.

"We need Cardi right away!" a panicked MoMA employee yelled.

She could hear the crowd of more than 4,000 people chanting, "Cardi B! Cardi B! Cardi B!" She tucked her hair behind her ears and stepped toward the stage.

# How Cardi B's 'Bodak Yellow' Took Over the Summer

BY JON CARAMANICA | AUG. 23, 2017

CARDI B JUMPS eagerly and ferociously into her single "Bodak Yellow (Money Moves)," beginning to rap while the intro is still finishing up. From the outset, she's taunting at gale force, boasting about her Louboutins — "These expensive, these is red bottoms, these is bloody shoes/Hit the store, I can get 'em both, I don't wanna choose" — aiming her words at those who might have underestimated her, a former stripper turned Instagram celebrity from uptown New York, who has now become one of hip-hop's most thrilling new presences.

"Bodak Yellow" is Cardi B's first true hit, but it is by no means her introduction to the world. A few years ago, she became an uproarious force on Instagram for her frank sexual talk and her comically acerbic wit, and her casually wise and ground-level relatable videos became part of the app's lingua franca. That earned her a spot on the reliably raucous reality series "Love & Hip Hop: New York," though it was clear from the beginning that her personality was far too grand for that show's microdramas.

With encouragement from one of her managers, she took up rapping, and has released a pair of mixtapes that mold her off-the-cuff verve and improvised bon mots into something stickier. "Bodak Yellow" feels like one of her Instagram clips come to life, funny and self-aware and savage.

The song rose to No. 3 on the Billboard Hot 100 in only its seventh week of release, a rapid ascent for a relatively unknown performer (at least, not one best known for music) and also for a female rapper. In recent years, Nicki Minaj has gone as high on the charts, but typically with her more pop-leaning songs like "Super Bass" and "Bang Bang," or "Anaconda," which benefited from a provocative video. The white rapper Iggy Azalea reached No. 1 with her emphatic mimeographs.

Cardi B's "Bodak Yellow (Money Moves)" rose to No. 3 on the Billboard Hot 100 in only its seventh week of release.

But no female rapper has moved as quickly from street hit to chart topper, an assertive reframing of the pathways typically available to them. Trevor Anderson, a chart manager at Billboard focused on R&B and hip-hop, said, "We haven't seen a song from someone brand new go up the charts this quick since Meghan Trainor," noting that was typically the preserve of more established stars like Justin Bieber or Rihanna. That it happened "without a meme, without a dance, it makes it that much weirder," he added.

Indeed the success of "Bodak Yellow" most closely parallels the viral power of songs like Rae Sremmurd's "Black Beatles" and Migos's "Bad and Boujee," both of which topped the Hot 100 this year with strong boosts from the meme ecosystem. David Bakula, the senior vice president for industry insights at Nielsen Entertainment, said the Cardi B song's ascent most closely paralleled "Black Beatles," before the #MannequinChallenge propelled it to No. 1.

Cardi B, 24, has no supporting meme, at least not yet — she is her own engine, a forceful personality and a technician who's more suave than she seems. She raps as if she's pushing out each line with a vigorous heave. Guided by the blunt doom-and-gloom beat — produced by J White — she works in a palpable rhythm of inhale and exhale, making for an entrancing rhythm. She also adjusts her approach line by line, sometimes beginning before the beat, sometimes on the beat and sometimes after the beat. (The flow pattern takes Kodak Black's "No Flockin" as a jumping off point, but adds muscle and sass.)

Cardi B has a thick voice — she swells her syllables until they take up all available space, and moves on and off the beat stealthily. Generally, she chops up her lines into small pieces — "They see pictures, they say, 'Goals,' bitch, I'm who they tryna be" — making more entry points, turning each into a sort of mini-chorus.

In two months, "Bodak Yellow" has made a wide impact, the sort of crescendo that let her, in the same weekend this month, perform for the artistically minded coolhunters at MoMA PS1's Warm-Up Series, and at the Dominican Day Parade. (She is of Dominican and Trinidadian heritage.)

Those are two different segments of New York's music culture, and part of the reason Cardi B can move so effortlessly between them is that in a genre largely marked by heavy Southern inflections and intonations, she still speaks with the reassuring contours of New York street slang, filtered through a Spanish accent.

In this way, she's part of another larger movement influencing the pop chart. By a very relaxed reading, the top three songs on the Billboard Hot 100 all owe their success to the Spanish-speaking world: "Despacito," the reggaeton-lite hit by the Puerto Rican stars Luis Fonsi and Daddy Yankee, has been at No. 1 for 15 weeks (the second-longest run of all time); just below it at No. 2, "Wild Thoughts," DJ Khaled's collaboration with Rihanna and Bryson Tiller, is in essence a revision of "Maria Maria," which was a Billboard No. 1 hit for Santana in 2000. Mr. Anderson said that alignment most recalled certain weeks in 1999, a year in which Ricky Martin, Jennifer Lopez, Santana, Christina Aguilera and Enrique Iglesias all had songs reach the Top 10.

Mr. Bieber's addition to "Despacito" — an English-language star singing partly in Spanish — helped propel it to the top of the chart, but Cardi B might have a different approach in mind. This month, she released a Spanish remix of "Bodak Yellow" featuring the Dominican-American rapper Messiah, one of the key figures in the Latin trap movement. That genre — in essence, a Spanish-language version of American hip-hop — has been gaining popularity over the last couple of years, but it might be "Bodak Yellow" that gives it its breakout moment.

Soon after its release, Spanish-language radio stations began playing "Bodak Yellow," Mr. Bakula noted. That means that turning this English song Spanish may be the thing to take it to the top of the chart — a kind of reverse "Despacito" in the making.

# Cardi B Wins New York Fashion Week

BY VALERIYA SAFRONOVA | FEB. 14, 2018

EVERY SEASON at fashion week, there is that one guest, glowing serenely among the camera flashes, dressed in a custom outfit, placed in the perfect seat at multiple shows. One year it was a transformed Kim Kardashian West, clad in Balmain and Givenchy; another, it was Rihanna, pulling out looks on looks on looks several months before being named Puma's creative director.

Look further back, and there is Lil' Kim (such a fashion fixture that Alexander McQueen called her his "idol"), Madonna (topless at Jean Paul Gaultier in 1992) and Sarah Jessica Parker when "Sex and the City" was just becoming a thing. (It's now a thing of nostalgia, with bits of its theme song playing this week at show as diverse as Michael Kors and Vaquera.)

This season's guest-of-the-week award goes to Belcalis Almanzar, your friend Cardi B, the rapper, former "Love & Hip-Hop" star and Instagram-video queen, whose "Bodak Yellow" became the song of summer and reached No. 1 on the Billboard Hot 100 charts in September, the first chart topper for a solo female rapper in nearly 20 years.

In January, the 25-year-old landed five of her songs in Billboard's top 10 in the R&B and hip-hop category, beating the record set by Beyoncé. (If you doubt the catchiness of her lyrics, listen to "Bartier Cardi" and try getting "wanna party with Cardi" out of your head afterward.)

Now Cardi B has become New York Fashion Week's darling, with appearances at key shows: There she was in a lush green jumpsuit at Christian Siriano, a white fur throw over her shoulder and jewels encrusting her daggerlike nails; at Prabal Gurung in a coatdress and mesh heels; at Jeremy Scott in an oversize black-and-white fur coat with newspaper cutouts printed all over it and white knee-high boots; and at Alexander Wang, in a black-and-tan trench coat, a black turban

Cardi B (on phone) sitting in the front row at the Jeremy Scott show during New York Fashion Week.

wrapped around her hair, chatting with Anna Wintour, a pairing that briefly set the internet on fire.

This New York Fashion Week is certainly not Cardi B's first, but her style credentials have grown significantly since September's New York shows. In an interview with Cosmopolitan magazine in December, Kollin Carter, who has been Cardi B's stylist since the spring, said that for a period of time, some labels refused to dress his client. All that is shifting.

"Most definitely it has changed from the beginning until now," Mr. Carter said. "Roberto Cavalli just started lending. Versace has been lending the past couple of times. Certain names are finally coming around."

With Mr. Carter at her side, Cardi B has caught fashion's eye with sleeker takes on the flashy style she established early on, and with showstopping looks like the floaty white butterfly Ashi dress that she wore for the Grammys red carpet, or the massive pastel blue Christian Siriano gown she wore to Rihanna's annual charity event, the Diamond Ball.

Since September, the rapper has been on the cover of not only Rolling Stone, Billboard and New York magazines, but also of more fashion-focused publications like Carine Roitfeld's CR Fashion Book and i-D magazine. The next stop — let's get this Cardi party on the cover of Vogue, right? — seems obvious.

# Cardi B Is a New Rap Celebrity Loyal to Rap's Old Rules on 'Invasion of Privacy'

BY JON CARAMANICA | APRIL 10, 2018

CARDI B's two breakthrough singles — "Bodak Yellow," which went to No. 1 on the Billboard Hot 100 last year, and "Bartier Cardi" — posited the Bronx social media savant turned-reality-TV scene-stealer turned rapper as a pugilist preaching the virtues of triumphing over difficult circumstances, the power of sexual agency and the satisfying payoff of hard work. She sounded ecstatic, and also ready for a rumble at any turn.

And so "Be Careful," the third single from her major-label debut album, "Invasion of Privacy," was a heady swerve. The beat is a tinkle, not a gloomy horror soundtrack, and even though Cardi is rapping with ferocity, she's also stepping gingerly; the subject is her heart, and she doesn't want to fracture it. At the bridge, she interpolates Lauryn Hill's "Ex-Factor," and she sings the hook with an enchanting rawness. That she's not a trained singer is the thing — she's most effective at her most unvarnished.

Cardi B moves seamlessly between these modes — taking a gut punch one moment, delivering one the next. She is more versatile than most rappers or pop stars of any stripe. And what's most promising about the exuberant and impressive "Invasion of Privacy" — an album full of thoughtful gestures, few of them wasteful — is that it's a catalog of directions Cardi, 25, might go in, slots she might fill, or even invent.

Much as Cardi B's ascent to music stardom has been unconventional, so is her approach to maintaining her place there. The Cardi of this concise and purposeful album is as confident on the breezy trap anthem "Drip" (featuring Migos, which includes her fiancé, Offset) as on the power-of-positive-thinking sermon "Best Life," featuring sermonizer Chance the Rapper. "I Like It," featuring the Puerto Rican rapper-singer Bad Bunny and the Colombian lite-reggaeton star J Balvin, is undeniable, both for its smoothness and also its revising of "I Like It Like That," the boogaloo classic by Pete Rodriguez.

Here alone are three possible Cardis: switchblade Cardi, empowerment-seminar Cardi, pan-Latin-unifier Cardi. And those aren't even all of them. On "She Bad" and "I Do," she raps about sex with the assertiveness and raw detail of Lil' Kim or Too Short. And on "Thru Your Phone," she's convincingly broken by an untrustworthy partner: "I might just cut all the tongues out your sneakers/ Smash your TV from Best Buy/You gon' turn me into Left Eye."

"Invasion of Privacy" is also, notably, a hip-hop album that doesn't sound like any of its temporal peers: It is not a samey post-trap longread designed for zoned-out maximal streaming, nor does it flirt with the sonic and thematic excesses of the SoundCloud generation. In fact, it's more reminiscent of the late 1990s and early 2000s, when New York rap was beginning to test its pop edges.

And though it's a debut album, it's by no means a debut: Cardi B has been famous for years already, first as a libertine social-media slice-of-life comic, and later as an effervescently campy reality-television standout. Both of those sorts of fame are relatively young, though. Succeeding in music has generally been thought to require something more than the natural vim and charm that she's deployed to this point.

And yet, that is partly a hip-hop myth deployed by gatekeepers. Cardi proves it's a lie: The skills she has been deploying to hilarious effect in her other careers are exactly the ones that make her music so invigorating. Few artists of any kind are so visibly and infectiously enthused.

As a result, the appetite for her is insatiable, and the career milestones are coming fast and furious: co-hosting "The Tonight Show" alongside Jimmy Fallon, appearing on the covers of various magazines, announcing her pregnancy during a performance on "Saturday Night Live."

She has also been the most reliable hip-hop guest star of the last 12 months, with appearances on G-Eazy's "No Limit," Migos's "MotorSport," Ozuna's "La Modelo" and the remix of Bruno Mars's "Finesse" — she has yet to release a dud. For someone who only started rapping a few years ago, that stylistic versatility is striking — it shows Cardi to be a quick study. And indeed, in a recent interview with Ebro Darden for Apple's Beats 1, she spoke openly about wanting to improve as a rapper and working with a more experienced rapper and songwriter, Pardison Fontaine, to improve her technical skills. "I needed a little bit of help from breaking out of my box," she said. "I need to learn how to flow a little bit easier and cleaner." (There was some consternation online after an old video of Mr. Fontaine performing part of "Be Careful" recently resurfaced online. Atlantic Records did not make songwriting credits for "Invasion of Privacy" available.)

The hard work shows, especially in terms of her cadences, and her ease in adapting to various production styles. Her quick-jab rhymes aren't particularly complex, but occasionally she gets off a delicious turn of phrase, like this one, from "Money Bag": "These bitches salty, they sodium, they jelly, petroleum/Always talking in the background, don't never come to the podium."

The work of becoming a great rapper is something that's rarely spoken about, but Cardi has been open about her education process, an implicit acknowledgment that her path to success has been unusual. It is one way rap stars are made today, and may be for the foreseeable future — not by triumphing over other rhymeslingers in Darwinian fashion, but by arriving to the genre as a fully formed personality, and then learning how to shrink-wrap that personality around beats.

This is a new paradigm, one that puts charm before bona fides. It is what happens when a genre is exposed to sunlight and expands beyond the internal logic that once drove it. But it's not enough for Cardi to win on those terms — she wants to succeed on the old ones, too.

# Cardi B Becomes the Fifth Female Rapper With a No. 1 Album

BY BEN SISARIO | APRIL 16, 2018

LAST SUMMER, with her ubiquitous hit "Bodak Yellow," Cardi B became the first female rapper since Lauryn Hill in 1998 to reach No. 1 on the Billboard singles chart with a fully solo release — that is, with no "feature" appearance by another artist (say, a male rapper).

Now, Cardi B has pulled off a similar feat on the album chart, as her "Invasion of Privacy" (KSR/Atlantic) opens at No. 1 with the equivalent of 255,000 album sales in the United States, according to Nielsen. As Billboard noted, she is only the fifth female rapper in history to top the chart, after Nicki Minaj, Eve, Foxy Brown and Ms. Hill.

"Invasion of Privacy" also had the highest streaming week ever for a female artist, with 202.6 million streams of tracks from the album, beating Beyoncé, who logged 115 million for "Lemonade" two years ago. In addition to the streams, "Invasion of Privacy" had 103,000 sales as a complete album, on formats like CD and download.

Also this week, Thirty Seconds to Mars, the rock band featuring the actor Jared Leto, opened at No. 2 with "America," and the Weeknd's new EP "My Dear Melancholy," which started at No. 1 last week, fell to No. 3. The soundtrack to "The Greatest Showman" is in fourth place, and XXXTentacion's "?" is No. 5.

# In the Name of Cardi, Let Us Pray

BY CAITY WEAVER | MAY 8, 2018

CLOTHED IN A 30-POUND pearl-encrusted dress the color of cream made of gold, a faintly lustrous silk duchesse satin overskirt that billowed like summer cumulus, gem-covered gloves that stretched to the shoulder, a jeweled halo headpiece, a thick buckle-and-pearl choker and colossal pearl drop earrings that clamped firmly to her ears on the backs of grinning gleaming putti, Cardi B communed with God in her hotel suite for 40 seconds.

Technically, the faintly lustrous silk duchesse satin overskirt was still being affixed to her at the instant of communion by a knelt helper fastening a semicircle of hooks and eyes around her waist. But time was running out (technically, time had run out 30 minutes earlier). And so, even though the Bronx-born rapper and self-identified Catholic might have preferred to be untweaked and unjostled during her moment of devotion, allowances had to be made.

The prayer of thanksgiving was led by her publicist, Patientce Foster.

"Thank you for Jeremy Scott," said Ms. Foster, her voice rushing out with the calm efficiency of a cool brook. Mr. Scott, Cardi's date for the Met Gala last night, and, as the creative director of Moschino, the man responsible for her tulle and wool and buckles and gems, was standing behind Cardi, reverently running the tips of his fingers across the satin overskirt as she shut her eyes in silent prayer.

"We appreciate our friendship with Moschino," said Ms. Foster, to God. "We ask that this night be successful, Lord. That you grace her feet, that you grace her presence, Lord. That she walks the carpet with everything that she has, Lord. That she gives everything that she has. We ask all these blessings in your name. Amen."

"Amen," said Cardi B, designing an invisible cross in the air above her slightly sparkling face.

"Okurrr!" added a few members of Cardi's team, filling the room in the Carlyle Hotel with the sounds of an avian chorus. ("Okurrr," with a trilled r, is one of Cardi's signature exclamations. The association of Cardi with "okurrr" has become so strong that the hotel embroidered the interjection on one of her room's pillowcases.)

One year ago, Cardi's sensational single "Bodak Yellow" had not yet been released, and she had to watch her more famous boyfriend (now fiancé) Offset, of the rap group Migos, dress for an ultraexclusive event to which she had never been invited. This year, on the 70th anniversary of the gala, she is, in the words of Mr. Scott, "obviously the girl that everyone's after. She's that new appointed pop princess. Diva, soon to be queen."

That Cardi's first Met Gala should fall on a night honoring the Costume Institute's exhibition "Heavenly Bodies: Fashion and the Catholic Imagination" was serendipitous, given her tremendous affection for God. Her brief to Mr. Scott was that her gown be "very religious"

Cardi B gets ready for the Met Gala, at the Carlyle Hotel in Manhattan in May 2018.

and "very luxurious." She was pleased that the final result reminded her of papal finery.

"Popes wear big things with rubies and gems," she explained, perhaps picturing less of a Pope Francis than one of those Medici popes, like the profligate Leo X, whose endorsement of the sale of indulgences led Martin Luther to instigate the Protestant Reformation.

Mr. Scott, who frequently dresses Cardi in bold retro rainbow colors for performances, said her outfit was "very inspired by Vatican tapestries — the whole, kind of, embroidery of deities." The dramatic coronal headpiece was meant to evoke the Virgin Mary.

"You know," said Mr. Scott, "like Mary, she is pregnant. But she know who the baby daddy is."

The dazzling companion suit to Cardi's outfit, sported by Mr. Scott at the Gala, was originally intended to be worn by Offset. Then, after work had begun on the custom wool and pearl motorcycle jacket/tuxedo coat hybrid (with matching trousers), it was decided that all three members of Migos would, in fact, attend the party as guests of Versace, whose chief designer Donatella Versace was one of the Met Gala's co-chairs. Fortunately, the trim Mr. Scott is roughly the same size as Offset. Like the priceless vestments passed down through centuries currently on display in the exhibit, the ensemble was handed down to him.

Although Cardi seemed happy to attend the party as Mr. Scott's date, dismay at the Versace intervention lingered. An hour or so before her official gala entrance, a blend of deep red lipsticks was painstakingly applied to her frown while she sat, robed, in a chair, and worried over Offset's replacement outfit.

"It's like, if y'all got so much people going with y'all, y'all could have just let him walk with me and take the two boys," she said, referencing Versace's extra-long list of guests (which included Katy Perry, Kim Kardashian West and Tom Brady) and the other two members of Migos: Takeoff and Quavo. The circumstances, she said, had left her "upset."

"That's why my baby ain't never gonna stand out," she said quietly.

"What do you mean?" asked Ms. Foster, who was floating around the room checking on every single element of everything, while simultaneously coordinating Cardi's schedule for the next day, and occasionally breaking into song. "Like, stand out on his own?"

"Not even on his own," said Cardi. "It's just like, I know how he wants to be."

(All three members of Migos eventually appeared on the Met's steps in matching color-coordinated Atelier Versace tuxedos.)

One baby that would stand out at the Met Gala was the fetus currently gestating inside Cardi. Mr. Scott said he designed her dress to "gloss over her, which is what I thought would be best for her figure." The snug fit and high belt emphasized her round stomach, even if the individual hand beading proved a little cumbersome for an expectant woman.

"Extremely heavy," is how Cardi characterized her outfit. "The beading is just crazy, and then," she said, cradling her midsection, "shorty weighs three and a half pounds." This news was met with laughs of delight from those assembled. "She do," said Cardi. "She do weigh three and a half pounds. That's pretty good for seven months, right?" she asked, looking around. "Because I was born five pounds."

The atmosphere inside the hotel suite cycled quickly between rapture and rupture. Ms. Foster and Cardi's warm, lanky stylist, Kollin Carter, led goofy champagne toasts (in which the pregnant rapper did not partake). Cardi excitedly recounted past Met Gala themes, recalling their chronology better than anyone in the room. But her mood plummeted when she was alerted to the fact that a fan-run Instagram account had posted a video of a recent confrontation involving herself, a member of her security team and a fan in Las Vegas. She expressed her frustration with a torrent of harsh words, many of them criticizing the security guard who, she argued, had inflamed the situation. She watched the video multiple times on her phone, becoming increasingly irritated with every replay. She asked Ms. Foster to contact the fan account and request its owner remove the video.

Cardi B poses before leaving her room at the Carlyle Hotel.

The bustling room fell silent, save for the furious clicks of Cardi's nails against iPhone glass, as, amid this social media Sturm und Drang, Mr. Scott's towering headpiece was gently positioned atop her head. There was nervous speculation about the best way to fasten it in place using the provided set of combs and ribbon ties. People half-joked about being afraid to hold the fragile object. It was a jeweled retaining wall barely holding back cascading black waves of hair.

"I feel like that's perfect," said Ms. Foster, after a series of minute adjustments.

Immediately, the crown fell.

For a moment, Cardi said nothing. She could say nothing, for the incredibly delicate and expensive headpiece was smushed up against her carefully painted lips. As it was lifted, she declared to the room with cold, quiet fury, "This is why I said matte lipstick. 'Cause it smudge."

She was correct: Her lipstick had smudged. None of the beadwork had broken, but a few perfectly white pearls had been stained pink. Ms. Foster began individually swabbing them clean with Q-Tips.

A judiciously placed FaceTime call from Cardi's younger sister, Hennessy, lifted her mood tremendously. "Slay!" Hennessy screamed through the speaker as she admired Cardi's gown. "Slay!" The effect was of air whipped into a meringue.

"I wanna cry!" exclaimed Cardi giddily a few moments later, as holes were snipped in her jeweled gloves so that her jeweled nails could poke through. A handshake with her at this point felt like a handshake with a very expensive lizard. She turned to Ms. Foster. "You don't wanna cry?"

"I wanna drink," said Ms. Foster. She poured herself a glass of champagne. (Celebratory.)

Cardi's voluminous skirt took up most of the cramped hotel elevator. It took up most of wherever she was, in fact. After wading through a crowd of screaming onlookers gathered outside the hotel to see a celebrity, any celebrity, she was forced to stand in the extra-large van hired to transport her the few blocks from the hotel to the Metropolitan Museum of Art. When a member of the Moschino team asked "How you doin', Mama?" Cardi responded "Ah?" She was unable to turn her body around, or swivel her head to see past her mass of hair, to determine the source of the question.

"Who's talking to me right now?" she asked with a laugh.

Cardi practiced her pose, which was: hands at sides. As the automobile crawled slowly forward, she was able, by a series of very meticulous adjustments, to position herself so that she was kneeling on the first row of back seats, facing out the rear window. Through careful manipulation of her embellished gloves and dagger sharp acrylic nails bearing more jewels than the earth's crust, she entered her iPhone's passcode. She began refreshing the hashtag #CardiB on Instagram, anxious to see how her dress had looked on the seconds-long walk from the hotel to the van, and to glean people's reactions to it.

"You don't want —" she began, and cut herself off, scrolling nervously through search results. (As well as countless posts recycling the same few images from her short stroll, the hashtag also revealed occasional spam of nude strangers.) "The first picture goes viral. Always. And you don't want the first picture to be terrible."

Mercifully, Cardi had only a few minutes to stress about the quality of the first frantic photos of herself and Mr. Scott. Less than half a mile later, it was time for her real trial: Getting her dress out of the van.

# CHAPTER 6

# Kanye West

Kanye West is one of the most acclaimed and controversial
hip-hop stars in the industry. Over the span of his 25-year
career, he has put out a half-dozen records, developed
a fashion label and married Kim Kardashian, becoming
one of America's most prominent celebrities. Kanye has
publicly dealt with mental illness and has received both
praise and condemnation for his off-the-cuff and unpredictable remarks. The articles in this section show both his
successes and his struggles.

## Kanye West, Flaunting Pain Instead of Flash

BY JON CARAMANICA | NOV. 24, 2008

"DO YOU REALLY have the stamina," Kanye West wonders to himself on
"Pinocchio Story (Freestyle Live From Singapore)," the bizarre rap-
star-in-need-of-a-Geppetto hidden track from his fourth album, "808s
& Heartbreak," "for everybody that sees you crying/And says, 'You
oughta laugh! You oughta laugh!' ?"

Oughtn't he, though? Mr. West is mouthy, impertinent, flamboyant,
bellicose, provocative, greedy and needy. But he is also funny, something, given his profound sense of entitlement, he very rarely gets
credit for.

On previous albums he's hilariously taken himself to task for his
foibles of style and narcissism. He rarely aims his daggers at others; there's plenty in the mirror to clown on. On "Breathe In, Breathe
Out," from his 2004 debut album, "The College Dropout," he distilled

the essential struggle that has defined his career into one sharp joke: "Always said if I rapped, I'd say something significant/But now I'm rapping about money, ho's and rims again."

On "808s & Heartbreak," which was released by Roc-A-Fella/Def Jam on Monday, Mr. West is done letting himself off the hook.

The product of a tumultuous year in his personal life, it operates solely on the level of catharsis — no commentary, no self-consciousness, no concern for anything but feeling. On "Pinocchio Story" he continues his lament:

*There is no Gucci I can buy*
*There is no Louis Vuitton to put on*
*There is no YSL that they could sell*
*To get my heart out of this hell*
*And my mind out of this jail*

On any of Mr. West's earlier albums, he would have quickly undermined this sentiment — of course a shopping spree would cheer him up — but here, bluntness is the goal. And so, as he's dismantling his storytelling structures, he's also making his productions skeletal, and largely trading bombastic rapping for vulnerable singing.

"808s & Heartbreak" sounds like none of his other albums, nor any rap album of note — "minimal but functional" is how he has described it to MTV. At best, it is a rough sketch for a great album, with ideas he would have typically rendered with complexity, here distilled to a few words, a few synthesizer notes, a lean drumbeat. At worst, it's clumsy and underfed, a reminder that all of that ornamentation served a purpose. After all, what is Kanye West without scale?

Mr. West would have been forgiven for taking a break after releasing "Graduation," his third album, last year. His mother, Donda West, died last November following complications from plastic surgery. In April Mr. West split from his fiancée, Alexis Phifer. By any measure, these are seismic changes, yet he persisted with recording.

Some of the results suggest his old, oversize sound. On both "Love Lockdown" and "Coldest Winter," thunderous drums cut through an electro haze, and "Bad News" features one of the most efficient bass lines Mr. West has ever constructed. "Amazing," a visceral collaboration with Young Jeezy, sounds as if it were recorded inside a whirring old grandfather clock, a collection of precisely moving parts neatly interlocking — classic Kanye.

Mr. West has cited the electro-pop pioneer Gary Numan and T J Swan, who sang exuberant, nasal hooks on many a 1980s Queens rap track, as vocal reference points for this album, though in truth hearing Mr. West try to sing these songs is far weirder.

Still, it is not quite sui generis. Early New Edition comes to mind. And in places, especially on the breezy, slick "Paranoid," this music is redolent of the chilly, slightly irregular R&B the producers the Neptunes were making four or five years ago, for Kelis, Omarion and others. Their synth-driven electro had blasts of funk momentum. But Mr. West uses electro (the title's "808" refers to the Roland TR-808 drum machine) for its sparseness, so that he might emote unchallenged.

Flaunting pain requires a sort of arrogance, too, so it's little surprise that Mr. West takes to it so naturally. Every song on the album is rife with anguish, and his lyrics, about the shards of broken relationships, though often tediously written, can carry a fresh sting.

"Let me ask you how long have you known dude," he raps on "Bad News." "You played it off and act like he's brand new/When did you decide to break the rules?" And the mistrust goes both ways.

"I know of some things that you ain't told me," he says on "Heartless." "I did some things, but that's the old me."

And it's not just the songs that are unmediated; much about this album's release suggested a lack of filters. Mr. West gave the premiere of the first single, "Love Lockdown," at the MTV Video Music Awards in September. Then various versions, with incremental tweaks, were leaked online. (One time, on his blog, kanyeuniversecity.com — Mr. West both blogs and Twitters — he drew attention to the "newer artwork with perfected type 4 all design snobs.") His self-control has faltered too: he has been arrested twice in recent months for tangles with the paparazzi, though charges were not filed in either incident.

For Mr. West, who has always intensely policed his own image, these are shocking ruptures. But they feel nominal up against much of this album, which has the immediacy, looseness and rambling quality of a venting session recorded into a Webcam and posted on YouTube.

Two songs, "Say You Will" and "Bad News," stretch out with instrumental breakdowns long past their obvious conclusion point, as if Mr. West forgot he left his sequencer on. On "Paranoid" you can actually hear laughing in the background, though whether it's at or with Mr. West, it's tough to say.

In an earlier era these would have been demo tapes, left in a vault to await exhumation for an anniversary edition. Now they are the official record, uncertain melodies, banal lyrics and all.

For years Mr. West fought the notion that he was a producer trying to rap. Now he's an underdog once more, a rapper who wants to sing.

But at the moment, Mr. West can't sing, and it is that weakness for which this album will ultimately be remembered, some solid songs notwithstanding. For him, using Auto-Tune, the pitch-correction software with the robotic vocal effect, is a true crutch. T-Pain, who has popularized it, can actually hold a tune, which makes the effect more of an accent and less the language itself.

No less a branding visionary than 50 Cent, whom Mr. West last year famously outsold in head-to-head first-week record sales, has criticized Mr. West's direction on this album, telling MTV, "I don't think the public will forgive him for it." (He added, "I think his album is T-Pain's record, but I'd rather buy it from T-Pain.") 50's wrong on at least one count, though: Mr. West's fans aren't loyal to form, they're loyal to him.

But Mr. West is testing that commitment. For all his self-scrutiny, he has never truly demanded emotional investment. Enjoying his music essentially means enjoying watching someone turn a lens on himself. How Mr. West filters, it turns out, is more compelling than how he feels.

# Behind Kanye's Mask

BY JON CARAMANICA  |  JUNE 11, 2013

MALIBU, CALIF. — From Shangri-la Studio here you can see the Pacific Ocean just over the fence lapping calmly at Zuma Beach. And this compound is just as Zen, with recording equipment set up in various locations, including an old bus and a spotless white house with all the mirrors removed.

But there is no rest at Shangri-la, at least for Kanye West. For several days in late May and early June, he and a rotating group of intimates, collaborators and hangers-on were holed up in service of finishing "Yeezus" (Roc-A-Fella/Def Jam), Mr. West's sixth solo album, out Tuesday, and one that marks a turn away from his reliable maximalism to something more urgent and visceral.

The original studios were built under the supervision of Bob Dylan and the Band in the 1970s — some of "The Last Waltz" was filmed here — and the property was bought in 2011 by the producer Rick Rubin, the man whose brain Mr. West had come here to pick. Together, they sandpapered off the album's rough edges, rerecording vocals and sometimes writing entire new verses. Even as the deadline loomed, Mr. West made room for an appearance at the baby shower for his girlfriend, Kim Kardashian, who's expecting their first child. As the days passed, the songs noticeably morphed, becoming more skeletal and ferocious.

One afternoon, Mr. Rubin exited the studio and declared, to everyone and no one, "It's un-bee-leave-able what's happening in there."

If by that he meant the paring-down to what Mr. West lightheartedly referred to as "aspiration minimalism," then yes, it was somewhat unbelievable.

Mr. West has had the most sui generis hip-hop career of the last decade. No rapper has embodied hip-hop's often contradictory impulses of narcissism and social good quite as he has, and no producer has celebrated the lush and the ornate quite as he has. He has spent most of his career in additive mode, figuring out how to make music that's majestic and thought-provoking and grand-scaled. And he's also widened the genre's gates, whether for middle-class values or high-fashion and high-art dreams.

At the same time, he's been a frequent lightning rod for controversy, a bombastic figure who can count rankling two presidents among his achievements, along with being a reliably dyspeptic presence at award shows (when he attends them).

But Mr. West is, above all, a technician, obsessed with sound, and the music of "Yeezus" — spare, direct and throbbing — is, effectively, a palate cleanser after years of overexertion, backing up lyrics that are among the most serrated and provocative of his career.

In a conversation that spanned several hours over three days, and is excerpted here, the Chicago-raised Mr. West, 36, was similarly forthright, both elliptical and lucid, even as long workdays led to evident fatigue. He compared the current moment — about to release "Yeezus," and looking to make a bigger footprint in worlds outside of music — to life just before his debut album, "The College Dropout," from 2004, another time when he was in untested waters. "I want to break the glass ceilings," he said. "I'm frustrated."

**Q:** *When your debut album, "The College Dropout" came out, the thing that people began to associate with you besides music was: Here's someone who's going to argue for his place in history; like, "Why am I not getting five stars?"*

**A:** I think you got to make your case. Seventh grade, I wanted to be on the basketball team. I didn't get on the team, so that summer I practiced. I was on the summer league. My team won the championship; I was the point guard. And then when I went for eighth grade, I practiced and I hit every free throw, every layup, and the next day I looked on this chart, and my name wasn't on it. I asked the coach what's up, and they were like, "You're just not on it." I was like, "But I hit every shot." The next year — I was on the junior team when I was a freshman, that's how good I was. But I wasn't on my eighth-grade team, because some coach — some Grammy, some reviewer, some fashion person, some blah blah blah — they're all the same as that coach. Where I didn't feel that I had a position in eighth grade to scream and say, "Because I hit every one of my shots, I deserve to be on this team!" I'm letting it out on everybody who doesn't want to give me my credit.

**Q:** *And you know you hit your shots.*

**A:** Yeah — you put me on the team. So I'm going to use my platform to tell people that they're not being fair. Anytime I've had a big thing that's ever pierced and cut across the Internet, it was a fight for justice. Justice. And when you say justice, it doesn't have to be war. Justice could just be clearing a path for people to dream properly. It could be clearing a path to make it fair within the arena that I play. You know, if Michael Jordan can scream at the refs, me as Kanye West, as the Michael Jordan of music, can go and say, "This is wrong."

**Q:** *You've won a lot of Grammys.*

**A:** "[My Beautiful] Dark [Twisted] Fantasy" and "Watch the Throne": neither was nominated for Album of the Year, and I made both of those in one year. I don't know if this is statistically right, but I'm assuming I have the most Grammys of anyone my age, but I haven't won one against a white person.

But the thing is, I don't care about the Grammys; I just would like for the statistics to be more accurate.

**Q:** *You want the historical record to be right.*

**A:** Yeah, I don't want them to rewrite history right in front of us. At least, not on my clock. I really appreciate the moments that I was able to win rap album of the year or whatever. But after a while, it's like: "Wait a second; this isn't fair. This is a setup." I remember when both Gnarls Barkley and Justin [Timberlake] lost for Album of the Year, and I looked at Justin, and I was like: "Do you want me to go onstage for you? You know, do you want me to fight" —

**Q:** *For you.*

**A:** For what's right. I am so credible and so influential and so relevant that I will change things. So when the next little girl that wants to be, you know, a musician and give up her anonymity and her voice to express her talent and bring something special to the world, and it's time for us to roll out and say, "Did this person have the biggest thing of the year?" — that thing is more fair because I was there.

**Q:** *But has that instinct led you astray? Like the Taylor Swift interruption at the MTV Video Music Awards, things like that.*

**A:** It's only led me to complete awesomeness at all times. It's only led me to awesome truth and awesomeness. Beauty, truth, awesomeness. That's all it is.

**Q:** *So no regrets?*

**A:** I don't have one regret.

**Q:** *Do you believe in the concept of regret?*

**A:** If anyone's reading this waiting for some type of full-on, flat apology for anything, they should just stop reading right now.

**Q:** *But that is something that you apologized for.*

**A:** Yeah, I think that I have like, faltered, you know, as a human. My message isn't perfectly defined. I have, as a human being, fallen to peer pressure.

**Q:** *So that was a situation in which you gave in to peer pressure to apologize?*

**A:** Yeah.

**Q:** *So if you had a choice between taking back the original action or taking back the apology, you'd take back the apology?*

**A:** You know what? I can answer that, but I'm — I'm just — not afraid, but I know that would be such a distraction. It's such a strong thing, and people have such a strong feeling about it. "Dark Fantasy" was my long, backhanded apology. You know how people give a backhanded compliment? It was a backhanded apology. It was like, all these raps, all these sonic acrobatics. I was like: "Let me show you guys what I can do, and please accept me back. You want to have me on your shelves."

**THE ALBUMS**

**Q:** *That's fascinating, to look at that record through that lens.*

**A:** I don't have some type of romantic relationship with the public. I'm like, the anti-celebrity, and my music comes from a place of being anti. That was the album where I gave people what they wanted. I don't think that at that point, with my relationship with the public and with skeptical buyers, that I could've done "Black Skinhead" [from "Yeezus"]

**Q:** *Does that make "Dark Fantasy" a dishonest album in some way?*

**A:** It's always going to be 80 percent, at least, what I want to give, and 20 percent fulfilling a perception. If you walk into an old man's house, they're not giving nothing. They're at 100 percent exactly what they want to do. I would hear stories about Steve Jobs and feel like he was at 100 percent exactly what he wanted to do, but I'm sure even a Steve Jobs has compromised. Even a Rick Owens has compromised. You know, even a Kanye West has compromised. Sometimes you don't even know when you're being compromised till after the fact, and that's what you regret.

I don't want to come off dissing "Dark Fantasy." It's me never being satisfied and then me coming and admitting and saying the truth. As much as I can air things out for other people, to air things out for myself, to say, "I feel like this could've been stronger."

**Q:** *It's interesting to think of that album as compromise, when it follows "808s & Heartbreak," which seemed very clearly to be the moment where you're like, "O.K., forget everything that's been expected of me."*

**A:** Yeah, people asked me to change my name for that album.

**Q:** *Like, label people?*

**A:** Yeah, different people. They said, "Do it under a different name." And when it came out, people used to be like, "Man, I wish it had more rapping on it." But I think the fact that I can't sing that well is what makes "808s" so special.

**Q:** *A fully trained professional singer couldn't have done that record. It just wouldn't have ever come out that way.*

**A:** Yeah. I love the fact that I'm bad at [things], you know what I'm saying? I'm forever the 35-year-old 5-year-old. I'm forever the 5-year-old of something.

**Q:** *A lot happened between "Graduation" and "808s," obviously: a lot of* *struggle, a lot of tough things for you. [Mr. West's mother died in 2007.]*

**A:** Creative output, you know, is just pain. I'm going to be cliché for a minute and say that great art comes from pain. But also I'd say a bigger statement than that is: Great art comes from great artists. There's a bunch of people that are hurt that still couldn't have made the album that was super-polarizing and redefined the sound of radio.

**Q:** *Do you feel like "808s" is the album of yours that has had the most impact?*

**A:** There are people who have figured out the exact, you know, Kanye West formula, the mix between "Graduation" and "808s," and were able to become more successful at it. "Stronger" was the first, like, dance-rap song that resonated to that level, and then "808s" was the first album of that kind, you know? It was the first, like, black new wave album. I didn't realize I was new wave until this project. Thus my connection with [the graphic designer] Peter Saville, with Raf Simons, with high-end fashion, with minor chords. I hadn't heard new wave! But I am a black new wave artist.

**Q:** *Was singing always something you wanted to do?*

**A:** I just dove more into rapping because I had a lot that I wanted to express, and I wasn't a really, really good singer.

**Q:** *Even though you had always wanted to be out in front, was there ever a point where you valued your anonymity?*

**A:** Yeah, I held on to the last moments of it. I knew when I wrote the line "light-skinned friend look like Michael Jackson" [from the song "Slow Jamz"] I was going to be a big star. At the time, they used to have the Virgin music [stores], and I would go there and just go up the escalator and say to myself, "I'm soaking in these last moments of anonymity." I knew I was going to make it this far; I knew that this was going to happen.

**Q:** *But producing happened for you first, especially after Jay-Z used you so heavily on "The Blueprint."*

**A:** I used to have tracks that sounded like Timbaland; I had tracks that sounded like [DJ Premier]. But Jay-Z was an amazing communicator that made the soul sound extremely popular. And because I could make the soul sound in my sleep, it finally gave me a platform to put the message that my parents put inside of me and that Dead Prez helped to get out of me and Mos Def and [Talib] Kweli, they helped to get out of me: I was able to put it, sloppily rap it, on top of the platform that Jay-Z had created for me.

Before, when I wanted to rap, my raps sounded like a bit like Cam'ron; they sounded a bit like Mase; they sounded a bit like Jay-Z or whoever. And it wasn't until I hung out with Dead Prez and understood how to make, you know, raps with a message sound cool that I was able to just write "All Falls Down" in 15 minutes.

**Q:** *Is that true?*

**A:** Yeah, that's how I discovered my style. I was just hanging out with them all the time in New York. I would produce for them. You know, I was able to slip past everything with a pink polo, but I am Dead Prez. And now, because I was able to slip past, I have a responsibility at all times.

**Q:** *What were the things that you were trying to do on "Late Registration" that you either did not or could not yet do on "Dropout"?*

**A:** I was trying to do different things with orchestras. It was just a vibe that I was trying to get at, a sound I was trying to mix with hip-hop to try to see how far I could expand it. I guess that was a Chicago thing, like Quincy Jones.

**Q:** *But you came here, you worked with Jon Brion [the Fiona Apple producer].*

**A:** I really liked the sound of some projects that Jon Brion had worked on. I was always considered this crazy hothead kid, but I would always just go and just really break bread with someone who I respected. I will completely bow to anybody I respect.

**Q:** *That era also includes what I find probably the most moving thing that you've ever done, which is calling out President Bush at the Hurricane Katrina telethon. To me, that moment is actually the peak of putting a message in a pop format, even though it's not a song.*

**A:** Yeah. I guess it's a very pop moment of a lifetime or generation. I mean, my dad's generation is a generation of messaging, you know? But that's just a piece of me being the opinionated individual that I am.

**Q:** *Were you conscious that that's what you were doing, or was it totally just instinct?*

**A:** Yeah, it was pretty bugged out. When you think about it, I was wearing like, a Juicy Couture men's polo shirt. We weren't there, like, ready for war.

**Q:** *I wonder if you see things in a more race-aware way now, later in your career, than you did then. The intensity of the feelings on "Watch the Throne" is much sharper.*

**A:** No, it's just being able to articulate yourself better. "All Falls Down" is the same [stuff]. I mean, I am my father's son. I'm my mother's child. That's how I was raised. I am in the lineage of Gil Scott-Heron, great activist-type artists. But I'm also in the lineage of a Miles Davis — you know, that liked nice things also.

**Q:** *On "Throne," who's in a darker mood on that record, you or Jay-Z?*

**A:** I'm always the one that's in a darker mood. And then also there was still a thing where I didn't feel comfortable, you know, going out on tour, the this, the that — all that by myself, yet. Like, I needed—

**Q:** *A buffer, kind of.*

**A:** I needed to connect with Jay.

**Q:** *Part of it was you wanting to have someone standing next to you and say, "He's cool. Ye's cool."*

**A:** Yeah, even with the kilt on.

**PUBLIC VERSUS PRIVATE**

**Q:** *You look at Jay or Diddy, and I'd say like, 90 percent of the time, you think they're having a good time. With you, I would say, I don't know, 50-50 maybe? Or 30-70?*

**A:** Maybe 90 percent of the time it looks like I'm not having a good time.

**Q:** *But you're in a very public relationship, a seemingly long and satisfying relationship: you're about to have a child.*

**A:** Any woman that you're in love with or that loves you is going to command a certain amount of, you know, energy. It's actually easier to focus, in some ways.

**Q:** *When you're uncertain about love, it can be such a distraction. It infects all the other areas.*

**A:** Yeah, that's what I mean when I say like, "Yo, I'm going to be super Zenned out like, five years from now." I'm the type of rock star that likes to have a girlfriend, you know? I'm the type of soul that likes to be in love and likes to be able to focus. And that inspires me.

**Q:** *On "Keeping Up With the Kardashians," there's a really affectionate scene where you go and help Kim sort through her clothes.*

**A:** That was from a place of love. It's hard when people read things in a lot of different ways. You know, the amount of backlash I got from it is when I decided to not be on the show anymore. And it's not that I have an issue with the show; I just have an issue with the amount of backlash that I get. Because I just see like, an amazing person that I'm in love with that I want to help.

**Q:** *Did you think differently about family after your mother passed?*

**A:** Yeah, because my mother was — you know, I have family, but I was with my mother 80 percent of the time. My mom was basically — [pause]

**Q:** *Was your family.*

**A:** Yeah, that's all I have to say about that.

**Q:** *What thoughts do you have about parenthood?*

**A:** That is a really interesting, powerful question. One of the things was just to be protective, that I would do anything to protect my child or my child's mother. As simple as that.

**Q:** *Have you ever felt as fiercely protective over anything as you are feeling now about those things?*

**A:** I don't want to explain too much into what my thoughts on, you know, fatherhood are, because I've not fully developed those thoughts yet. I don't have a kid yet.

**Q:** *You haven't experienced it yet.*

**A:** Yeah. Well, I just don't want to talk to America about my family. Like, this is my baby. This isn't America's baby.

## BIRTHING 'YEEZUS'

**Q:** *One of the things I thought when I heard the new record was, "This is the anti-'College Dropout.' " It feels like you're shedding skin. Back then, you were like: "I want more sounds. I want more complicated raps. I want all the things." At what point did that change?*

**A:** Architecture — you know, this one Corbusier lamp was like, my greatest inspiration. I lived in Paris in this loft space and recorded in my living room, and it just had the worst acoustics possible, but also the songs had to be super simple, because if you turned up some complicated sound and a track with too much bass, it's not going to work in that space. This is earlier this year. I would go to museums and just like, the Louvre would have a furniture exhibit, and I visited it like, five times, even privately. And I would go see actual Corbusier homes in real life and just talk about, you know, why did they design it? They did like, the biggest glass panes that had ever been done. Like I say, I'm a minimalist in a rapper's body. It's cool to bring all those vibes and then eventually come back to Rick [Rubin], because I would always think about Def Jam.

**Q:** *His records did used to say "reduced by Rick Rubin."*

**A:** For him, it's really just inside of him. I'm still just a kid learning about minimalism, and he's a master of it. It's just really such a blessing, to be able to work with him. I want to say that after working with Rick, it humbled me to realize why I hadn't — even though I produced "Watch the Throne"; even though I produced "Dark Fantasy" — why I hadn't won Album of the Year yet.

This album is moments that I haven't done before, like just my voice and drums. What people call a rant — but put it next to just a drumbeat, and it cuts to the level of, like, Run-D.M.C. or KRS-One. The last record I can remember — and I'm going to name records that you'll think are cheesy — but like, J-Kwon, "Tipsy." People would think that's like a lower-quality, less intellectual form of hip-hop, but that's always my No. 1. There's no opera sounds on this new album, you know what I mean? It's just like, super low-bit. I'm still, like, slightly a snob, but I completely removed my snob heaven songs; I just removed them altogether.

**Q:** *On this album, the way that it emphasizes bass and texture, you're privileging the body, and that's not snobby.*

**A:** Yeah, it's like trap and drill and house. I knew that I wanted to have a deep Chicago influence on this album, and I would listen to like, old Chicago house. I think that even "Black Skinhead" could border on house, "On Sight" sounds like acid house, and then "I Am a God" obviously sounds, like, super house.

**Q:** *Visceral.*

**A:** Yeah, visceral, tribal. I'm just trying to cut away all the — you know, it's even like what we talk about with clothing and fashion, that sometimes all that gets in the way. You even see the way I dress now is so super straight.

**Q:** *Does it take you less time to get dressed now than it did five years ago?*

**A:** Hell, yeah.

**Q:** *You look at your outfits from five or seven years ago, and it's like —*

**A:** Yeah, kill self. That's all I have to say. Kill self.

**Q:** *One of the things that you've thrived on over the years is sort of a self-conception as an outsider, that you're fighting your way in. Do you still, in this moment, feel like that?*

**A:** No, I don't think I feel like that anymore. I feel like I don't want to be inside anymore. Like, I uninvited myself.

**Q:** *What changed?*

**A:** I think just more actual self-realization and self-belief. The longer your 'gevity is, the more confidence you build. The idea of Kanye and vanity are like, synonymous. But I've put myself in a lot of places where a vain person wouldn't put themselves in. Like what's vanity about wearing a kilt?

**Q:** *But there's vanity in fashion. You make clothes, but some people think it's a vanity project, that you don't take it seriously.*

**A:** But the passion is for humanity. The passion is for people. The passion is for the 18-year-old version of myself. The passion is for the kids at my shows. I need to do more. I need to be able to give people more of what they want that currently is behind a glass. I don't believe that it's luxury to go into a store and not be able to afford something. I believe luxury is to be able to go into a store and be able to afford something.

I sat down with a clothing guy that I won't mention, but hopefully if he reads this article, he knows it's him and knows that out of respect, I didn't mention his name: this guy, he questioned me before I left his office:, "If you've done this, this, and this, why haven't you gone further in fashion?" And I say, "I'm learning." But ultimately, this guy that was talking to me doesn't make Christmas presents, meaning that nobody was asking for his [stuff] as a Christmas present. If you don't make Christmas presents, meaning making something that's so emotionally connected to people, don't talk to me.

**Q:** *But at the same time, this feels like the Grammy conversation, because what I keep thinking is: the people whose hands you're trying to shake, they may control certain corridors of power, but those aren't even the relevant corridors of power anymore.*

**A:** I'm a professional musician because I have the structure of Universal Records. I'm a professional creative. Since I did the Louis Vuitton sneaker, I've never been allowed to be in a continually creative structured place that makes product. I've had meetings where a guy actually told me, "What we're trying to figure out is how we can control you." In the meeting, to me! Why do you want to control me? Like, I want the world to be better! All I want is positive! All I want is dopeness! Why would you want to control that?

That's why I said "I throw these Maybach keys" [in the new song "New Slaves"]. I would rather sit in a factory than sit in a Maybach.

I want to tell people, "I can create more for this world, and I've hit the glass ceiling." If I don't scream, if I don't say something, then no one's going to say anything, you know? So I come to them and say, "Dude, talk to me! Respect me!"

**Q:** *Respect my trendsetting.*

**A:** Yeah, respect my trendsetting abilities. Once that happens, everyone wins. The world wins; fresh kids win; creatives win; the company wins.

I think what Kanye West is going to mean is something similar to what Steve Jobs means. I am undoubtedly, you know, Steve of Internet, downtown, fashion, culture. Period. By a long jump. I honestly feel that because Steve has passed, you know, it's like when Biggie passed and Jay-Z was allowed to become Jay-Z.

I've been connected to the most culturally important albums of the past four years, the most influential artists of the past ten years. You have like, Steve Jobs, Walt Disney, Henry Ford, Howard Hughes, Nicolas Ghesquière, Anna Wintour, David Stern.

I think that's a responsibility that I have, to push possibilities, to show people: "This is the level that things could be at." So when you get something that has the name Kanye West on it, it's supposed to be pushing the furthest possibilities. I will be the leader of a company that ends up being worth billions of dollars, because I got the answers. I understand culture. I am the nucleus.

# Kanye West's Year of Breaking Bad

BY JON CARAMANICA  |  JAN. 5, 2017

BACK AT THE BEGINNING of 2016, Kanye West was already sounding alarms. On Dec. 31, 2015, he released "Facts," an out-of-nowhere harangue that insulted Nike, praised his wife's business acumen and seemed to express sympathy for Bill Cosby. About a week later came "Real Friends," as potent and dispiriting a catalog of loneliness he has ever recorded, a song about how fame warps and traps, and no matter how high it brings you, will always yank you down.

These songs set the stage for one of the most productive, disjointed and confusing years in the life of Kanye. It was one that began with him seeking grace, in the form of music, and also ended that way, but for very different reasons, following his hospitalization and his meeting with the president-elect, Donald J. Trump. And yet the Kanye of

Kanye West performs during the opening of his Saint Pablo Tour in Indianapolis, Aug. 25, 2016.

12 months ago and the Kanye of today aren't so far apart: instability, loneliness, a sense that he was being treated unfairly, a continuing quest to be heard. Mr. West may be facing severe public scrutiny, skepticism and concern, but even during this most challenging stretch, there are clear bridges to his old self.

In the last year, he has been busy. He released an album, "The Life of Pablo," then continued to tweak it for a while in real time. He convened two runway collections of his Yeezy fashion line — one in Madison Square Garden, one in a park on Roosevelt Island. He had an art show in a Los Angeles gallery and teased a video game based on his mother's journey to heaven. He sold merchandise in a few dozen pop-up shops around the world and released several iterations of his signature sneaker. And he performed dozens of nights of a tour that remade the proportions of arena concerts.

Though there were bumps along the way — the uncertain rollout of "Pablo," the collapsing models (and shoe heels) at Roosevelt Island — the first nine months of the year were Mr. West firing on all pistons, and meeting with success.

But the final three months of 2016 spiraled well beyond his control. First came the robbery of his wife, Kim Kardashian, in Paris, a violent affair that included the theft of the 20-karat diamond engagement ring he gave her, worth a reported $4 million. That was followed by the disruption of his tour, and its eventual cancellation, following a couple of speeches in which he spoke admiringly of Mr. Trump; his involuntary admission to U.C.L.A. Medical Center hospital, followed by what will certainly be remembered as the most public crack of all: his meeting with Mr. Trump at Trump Tower on Dec. 13.

Rupture has long been the axis around which Mr. West's career has turned — where most artists seek to create smooth narratives about themselves and get everyone else to play along, he instead prefers disruptive leaps, quick reframing and firebrand positioning. Stasis is his kryptonite.

The ruptures are typically intentional provocations, but not always: The period of deep trauma following the 2007 death of his mother remains one of Mr. West's most vital, influential and least understood times. The last three months of 2016 figure to be another such stretch. Mr. West dyed his hair blond, then multiple colors. In paparazzi photos, and even in the holiday-party family picture he posted on Twitter, his eyes are somewhere far-off. Since his hospitalization, he has barely spoken publicly. When he and Mr. Trump descended to the Trump Tower lobby after their meeting, they were peppered with questions from the media, to which Mr. West replied only, "I just want to take a picture right now."

Mr. West's embrace of Mr. Trump, who spoke about black communities in cartoonish, inaccurate strokes ("They have no jobs, they have horrible education, they have no safety or security"), arrives at a particularly unlikely moment in his artistry. In 2013, he released "Yeezus," an album full of industrial thump that featured some of his most acidic political commentary. It struck a confrontational tone that Mr. West carried through that year and the next.

By contrast, "The Life of Pablo" takes a turn to the ornate, the melodic and also the emotionally intimate. "Ultralight Beam," the album opener, is a prayer. On songs like "Real Friends" and "No More Parties in LA," Mr. West sounds exhausted and exasperated, while "I Love Kanye" is a withering self-assessment passed off as a taunt ("I miss the old Kanye"). And on "FML," there was the specter of psychological instability, a possible foreshadowing of troubles to come: "You ain't never seen nothing crazier," he rapped, than him when he's "off his Lexapro."

The Saint Pablo tour, which began in August, took the worship elements of the album and rendered them literal. Each night, for a couple of hours, Mr. West performed while tethered to a platform that dangled over the crowd and moved from one end of the room to the other like a warship. The optics were bracing: Mr. West was both a god hovering over his subjects and a slave bound for their entertainment. Below him, chaos and thrill. Above him, klieg lighting that baked and beatified him. The approach was also a stark contrast to his last tour, following "Yeezus," which became well-known for lengthy speeches that veered between motivation and tirade.

But in November, that impulse began to return. In San Jose, he said, "If I would've voted, I would've voted on Trump." In Sacramento a few nights later, he spoke for about 15 minutes before leaving the stage having performed only three songs. The remainder of the tour was swiftly canceled, and a few days later, Mr. West was hospitalized, after the police were called to perform a welfare check after an episode at his personal trainer's home.

Mr. West's collapse was very public, but then again, even his private space is public: "My psychiatrist got kids that I inspired/First song they played for me was 'bout their friend that just died," he rapped on "No More Parties in LA." He still appears on his wife's reality show, "Keeping Up With the Kardashians." Plus, some of his most fascinating work last year — the video for the song "Famous," and the ensuing art installation — was about the erosion of the public-private boundary.

In the clip for the song — which restoked the tension between him and Taylor Swift — doubles of him, his wife, Ms. Swift, Mr. Trump, Rihanna, Mr. Cosby and more celebrities all lay in an oversized bed, nude. It was an outrageous gesture of invasion, but it was also disarmingly tender — here were the famous, the powerful, the protected, shown in innocent, vulnerable slumber. It felt like a wish more than an attack.

How Mr. West interacts with other celebrities — fearlessly, stubbornly — continues to be one of his most powerful tools. During his Sacramento speech, he accused Beyoncé of negotiating her way to a video of the year award at the MTV Video Music Awards last year, and in October, lashed out at Jay Z, his longtime mentor, about the tensions between Apple Music and Tidal, and how the two men's children "have never even played together." In this way, Mr. West makes art of his peers, too.

That's even more true of the younger generation. His most important mentor-mentee relationship is with Chance the Rapper, whose thumbprint is all over "The Life of Pablo." (He also appeared on Chance's "Coloring Book.") Lil Yachty, the smiling hip-hop provocateur then still at the beginning of his ascent, was a model in the Yeezy Season 3 show at the Garden, as was a lackadaisical Young Thug.

But to some from an older generation — Mr. West's elders, peers or his first wave of acolytes now grown up — Mr. West was floundering. Following Mr. West's embrace of Mr. Trump, Talib Kweli posted a series of emotional appeals on Twitter: "we love u. u r everything u say u are. A genius, an icon. U added greatness to my life. But lifting Trump up kills us. Come home." And in early December, J. Cole released "False Prophets," a song that, while not using Mr. West's name, appeared to be discussing Mr. West's Icarus-like career path: "When he tell us he a genius but it's clearer lately/It's been hard for him to look into the mirror lately." Sometimes the critiques came directly to Mr. West's doorstep. During the Sacramento speech, Mr. West singled out Q-Tip: "I love you, bro. Don't tell me how to be me, though."

The low points of last year, whether a sign of deep trouble or just a momentary misalignment, have caused a radical shift in how Mr. West is publicly received. His weeklong hospitalization, and the presumed illness that led to it, rendered him more sympathetic to critics, but his support of Mr. Trump was, to some, unforgivable. (That his behavior can cause offense is something he is warming to: Three times last year, he used his Twitter for damage control, an unfamiliar position.)

Embracing Mr. Trump is perhaps the most consequential political act of an artist who, at a much earlier and less sure-footed stage of his career, in the wake of Hurricane Katrina risked his mainstream acceptance to make a bold accusation on a national telethon: "George Bush doesn't care about black people."

But he and Mr. Trump have parallels — both are vocal about those who they see as obstacles; both are steadfast in their self-belief. Perhaps Mr. West sees in Mr. Trump someone who freely speaks his mind and has been rewarded for it. During his speech at the Sacramento show, Mr. West referenced him as a sort of spirit guide: "Yeah, I'm taking his lead. I'ma just say how I say, be 'Ye, and win."

Read another way, Mr. West's embrace of Mr. Trump — symbolic or otherwise — suggests an incipient nihilism at work. Rather than align himself with broader social causes — "I love being a voice of freedom when so many people are scared to speak up," he wrote on Twitter in February — or the mainstream of black political thought, or even the politics of his wife, a supporter of Hillary Clinton, Mr. West's unlikely shift suggests the maneuvers of someone who no longer believes in the systems that have previously nourished, sustained and inspired him — someone whose sense of safety has been revoked.

It should also be said, though, that Mr. West's sympathy for the publicly maligned is as central to his personality as his self-regard. His outspokenness in favor of Mr. Trump wasn't the first time he sided with a controversial figure — "Bill Cosby innocent!" he tweeted in February.

Bill Cosby, Donald Trump, Kanye West: highly visible stars with highly motivated antagonists. Mr. West may well perceive himself as still aligning with the persecuted, but the view from the top can be disorienting. It's one thing to side with those who suffer on the wrong end of power, but another thing altogether to side with the ones who wield it, consequences be damned.

# The Heartbreak of Kanye West

OPINION | BY DREAM HAMPTON | MAY 7, 2018

IT SEEMS SO LONG AGO, but it has been only a week since Mr. West came out of the closet as the same-dragon-loving, Trump-supporting, slave-shaming, alt-fact fire breather. Last weekend's "Saturday Night Live," hosted by the actor and musician Donald Glover, turned Mr. West's weeklong trolling into the horror film it felt like. But ending the week laughing at Mr. Glover's sendup of Mr. West hasn't made watching him unravel any less infuriating or heartbreaking.

Mr. West thought his recent return to Twitter after an almost yearlong hiatus, with relentless contrarian, stream-of consciousness tweets from the minuscule Negro corner of the alt-right world, would read like a takeover of Twitter. But that's not how the platform works. Black Twitter runs Twitter, and Black Twitter swiftly handed Mr. West his lunch. Mr. West was reading the blowback and did exactly what a person does when he or she is losing — he dug in.

Black Twitter had seen that show before when Mr. West posed for cameras in the lobby of Trump Tower in December 2016 after being hospitalized. The anger at the rapper was because he has allowed himself to be a useful idiot for a useful idiot.

Like Mr. Trump, who also brags about not reading books, Mr. West is parroting the racist right-wing talking points he has learned from watching YouTube videos. The same white power wing nuts who trolled him for years as a way of defending Taylor Swift's honor are now over the moon to hear the rapper blame President Barack Obama for not ameliorating gang violence in Chicago, to see Mr. West at the office of the gossip website TMZ blaming his own enslaved ancestors for their enslavement.

Because the trolls won the election, their dangerous drivel sometimes becomes policy, as the musician John Legend tried to tell Mr. West in a series of reasonable texts that Mr. West immediately published. Those talking points from Alex Jones and company perpetuate mass criminalization and incarceration, deportation and worse.

When a poll shows 20 percent of Trump supporters would have opposed the freeing of slaves, it's more than a fun punctuation ending the night on cable news. Those talking points run in tandem with textbooks used in Texas schools that describe slaves as "workers" and their journey to America as "immigration." The denial of the sadism and brutality of slavery is perpetuated when there's "another side" arguing to keep statues and symbols of the Confederacy in public places, and when plantation tours explain the generosity with which slave owners cared for their chattel.

When Mr. Legend and Mr. West later demonstrated their lasting friendship by publishing pictures of themselves at a baby shower "despite their differences," they advanced the fiction that theirs are two equal but divergent viewpoints. They are not. There is the same old white supremacy that denies black humanity, and there are people who struggle mightily against white supremacy and for black life.

It would be unfair to call Mr. West's public outbursts mere stunts. He was right about the MTV Video Music Awards best female video of 2009. Beyoncé should have won. Mr. West was at his most profound in 2005 when he said George Bush doesn't care about black people after that president did a flyby of the poor and black victims of New Orleans's levee failure.

When Hurricane Katrina happened, Mr. West was a new artist and his "College Dropout" was an album that helped give millennials a clear sense of identity. He wrote about being insecure, about not being comfortable managing his new money and visibility. That honesty was refreshing. His self-reflection and self-diagnosis felt familiar to a generation that drafted dozens of confessionals a day on social media.

Kids who were in high school and younger when Mr. West made his debut connected with him more than they did with M.C.s like

Jay-Z or even Tupac Shakur or Biggie Smalls, who deserve respect but belonged to another era. 50 Cent seemed a Neanderthal compared with the nerdy, backpack-wearing Mr. West.

Mr. West rose as the economy collapsed, and his open insecurity spoke to a generation whose struggle was the housing market collapse, not a crack epidemic. He is the son of a single mother, a professor who raised him abroad for a semester or two in China. His story was more like President Obama's than 50 Cent's.

This new generation didn't necessarily believe in crowns, but Mr. West was their guy, and almost immediately after being chosen, he began to collapse from the pressure.

We've seen Mr. West melt down before. His 2013 radio interview with the journalist Sway was as unhinged as Mr. Trump's recent call-in to "Fox & Friends." Mr. Trump and Mr. West both seemed to want the same thing in those tirades — to be recognized as gods. Mr. Trump roared into the phone about the Breitbart calculator he uses to argue voter fraud cost him the popular vote. The rapper screamed at Sway, who seemed unwilling to concede that Mr. West is the greatest artist of his generation. Or maybe Mr. West was arguing he was the greatest artist of any generation. It's hard to remember. We got a harmless new pop culture refrain from the interview — "How, Sway?" — and mostly moved on.

But unlike Mr. Trump's call, Mr. West's interview with Sway was videotaped. We were witnessing something more than his outsize ego doing battle with his mammoth insecurity. His refusal to make eye contact with Sway was particularly off-putting. He spent the hour talking to the heavens — not to the interviewer, not even to the audience. Absent was the wink and nod embedded in Muhammad Ali's news conference performances, where he talked about himself in the third person and invented the kind of braggadocio that would become hip-hop's bedrock. Watching Mr. West during that interview, some of us began to worry about his mental health.

Like most of his fans, I'm not qualified or interested in actually attempting to diagnose an illness in Mr. West. He has shared with us that he has been medicated and hospitalized. He has also told us that his recent Twitter rant is unconnected to his mental health, that he is fine. His performance at TMZ was similar to his interview with Sway. It wasn't until Van Lathan, on the staff there, interrupted to take him on about slavery that Mr. West even seemed present in the room, and that was truly heartbreaking to watch.

But what was dangerous was the way Mr. West included Candace Owens, an alt-right darling, a black woman and puppet, on his broadcast from the TMZ office. Her participation was most likely arranged by alt-right operatives. A Black Lives Matter strategist hypothesized as much on his Facebook page when he noticed white power operatives taking credit for connecting the two.

With uncharacteristic generosity, Mr. West ceded the mic to Ms. Owens, who allows a racist, misogynist movement to hold her up as evidence that it is neither. Mr. Trump's speechwriters made sure to include Mr. West in his recent speech to the National Rifle Association, thanking the rapper for "doubling" his approval numbers among black people. He was referring to a real poll, but he got it wrong. The doubling was only among black men, from 11 percent to 22 percent (with a margin of error of nine points).

Mr. West barely owned the entire week. R. Kelly had some karma delivered to his front door, and the fascist, feeble Rudy Giuliani had his moments, embarrassing himself. But Mr. West's shrill missives from the monochromatic sunken place that is his mansion may be consequential in ways he can't fathom.

**DREAM HAMPTON** (@dreamhampton) is a filmmaker and writer.

# Kanye West Writes a Song of Himself on 'Ye'

BY JON PARELES | JUNE 3, 2018

BAIT AND SWITCH was a typically savvy move for Kanye West, whose new EP-length album, "Ye" — seven songs, 23 minutes long — was released on Friday. His production skills are matched by his gift for self-promotion. The rollout has trolled and roiled social media over the past few weeks as Mr. West wore a red Make America Great Again cap, exulted that he and President Trump share "dragon energy" and told TMZ that 400 years of slavery "sounds like a choice." He also spoke in interviews about his hospitalization for mental problems in 2016, and about getting addicted to opioids after liposuction — topics that loom large on "Ye."

Mr. West's self-described "free thought" drew ample attention, including Twitter praise from the president and worries from hip-hop colleagues that his mental illness had worsened. The parallels between Mr. West and the president were clear. Both exploit the feedback loop of inflammatory statements and righteous reactions to stoke attention and present themselves as fearless. Both exult in fame and wealth and put feelings before facts. And both use contradictory pronouncements to cover all bases.

Before "Ye" appeared, Mr. West released an online single, "Ye vs. the People," that had him debating the rapper T.I. over the symbolism of the cap. After Mr. West insists he "wore it, rocked it, gave it a new direction," T.I. jabs, "You wore a dusty-ass hat to represent the same views/As white supremacy, man, we expect better from you," and goes on to add, "You're taking a bad idea and making it worse."

But politics have served largely as clickbait for the surprisingly slight "Ye," which is part of a promised string of seven-song albums produced by Mr. West: Pusha-T's "Daytona," which was released May 25, to be followed by a Kid Cudi-Kanye West collaboration and releases from Nas and Teyana Taylor. While Mr. West's previous releases have made musical leaps, "Ye" often comes across as a recap, revisiting the gospel mutations of his 2016 album "The Life of Pablo," the revamped sweet soul of "The College Dropout," the rock heft of "My Beautiful Dark Twisted Fantasy" and the stark synthesizers of "Yeezus."

On "Ye," Mr. West's focus is not on America but on his all-encompassing self-absorption: as a celebrity, a rapper enmeshed in beefs, a husband, a parent and a case study in bipolar disorder. The cover photo for "Ye" bears a handwritten message: "I hate being Bi-Polar its awesome."

The album whipsaws between grandiosity and anxiety, though Mr. West's self-regard easily prevails. "I got dirt on my name, I got white on my beard/I had debt on my books, it's been a shaky-ass year," Mr. West raps in "No Mistakes." But soon afterward, he goes on to taunt, "I don't take advice from people less successful than me."

Politics have served as a teaser for Kanye West's new album, "Ye," but America is not the subject of the seven-song LP, which he debuted at a listening party in Wyoming on Thursday.

It's the way Mr. West has always worked, bouncing confident assertions against his own questions, doubts and rebuttals. His hugely influential early production style found the sonic equivalent, deploying lush, nostalgia-triggering samples of vintage R&B hits and gospel affirmations against brittle new beats. He has since delved into ever more unexpected sources, sometimes abrasive and sometimes lavish; the sample credits on a Kanye West album are always far-flung and enlightening.

On his early albums Mr. West was an underdog, fighting through the kind of obstacles his listeners might share. Then fame both emboldened and isolated him. His productions stayed innovative, but his lyrics could turn petty and boorish — exacerbated, apparently, by the bipolar disorder that Mr. West has said he was diagnosed with at age 40. (He turns 41 on Friday.)

Mr. West's ups and downs dominate the songs on "Ye," which has a hint of narrative, ascending from private desolation to familial comfort, only to end with a twist. Mr. West opens the album with a thesis: "The most beautiful thoughts are always besides the darkest." The track is "I Thought About Killing You," much of which is a spoken-word recitation about murderous and suicidal impulses over a cappella voices intoning, "I know, I know."

In "Yikes," a pulsing, plunging synthesizer bass line and echoing, hooting voices accompany Mr. West as he raps about drugs and fears — "sometimes I scare myself." But he soon pivots to remark on the sexual misconduct accusations faced by the hip-hop mogul Russell Simmons and to boast about womanizing; at the end, he insists that being bipolar is a superpower, not a disability.

Mr. West brings up his "choice" comments in "Wouldn't Leave" — not as a historical argument, but as proof of his audacity: "I said slavery a choice, they said, 'How, Ye?'/Just imagine if they caught me on a wild day." As the song continues, it mixes self-praise — "I got the mind state to take us to the stratosphere" — with thanks to his wife for staying with him, even if he embarrasses her and his public posturing jeopardizes their wealth. The production is gospelly and comforting; all that matters is domestic loyalty.

Although the songs admit to infidelities, it grows clear by the end of "Ye" that Mr. West clings to his family. And the songs improve as he incorporates women's perspectives alongside his own. "Ghost Town" — built on thick, dramatic psychedelic guitar and organ build-ups sampled from Vanilla Fudge — is a montage of unfulfilled yearn-ings that culminates in the album's most striking cameo, from the New Jersey rapper and singer 070 Shake, who was 20 when the album came out. Battling apathy and numbness, she belts, "I put my hand on a stove to see if I still bleed/And nothing hurts anymore, I feel kind of free."

And in the album's final song, the hymnlike "Violent Crimes," Mr. West delivers an unambiguous mea culpa. Though the premise is shopworn — the father of a daughter suddenly realizes what women face from men — he's forced to reckon with his own behavior. "Father forgive me, I'm scared of the karma/'Cause now I see women as some-thing to nurture, not something to conquer." He longs to keep his daughter protected and strong against "pimps" and "monsters" and "playas"; he worries about what she'll have to face. Mr. West still has a streak of compassion and empathy, in the rare moments when he's not thinking only of himself.

# Glossary

**aesthetics**  Of or relating to beauty or physical appearance.

**beatboxing**  A musical style or technique, especially in hip-hop, in which the sounds and rhythms of percussion instruments or a drum machine are simulated by using the mouth and voice.

**contrarian**  Opposing or rejecting popular opinion; going against current practice.

**ethnomusicologist**  A professional who studies music from a cultural and social perspective.

**freestyle**  The art of vocal improvising, particularly of a rap.

**gangster rap**  Rap music with lyrics explicitly portraying the violence and drug use of urban gang life.

**Gucci**  An Italian luxury fashion brand. In slang, it refers to something highly coveted or good.

**hustler**  An aggressively enterprising person.

**meme**  An element of a culture, specifically a humorous image, video or piece of text, that is copied and passed from one individual to another.

**persona**  A role or character adopted by an author or an actor.

**platinum**  A certification in the music industry that indicates an album has sold a million copies.

**racism**  Prejudice, discrimination or antagonism directed against someone of a different race based on the belief that one's own race is superior.

**rap music**  A type of music in which the words are not sung but are spoken in a rapid, rhythmic way.

**reggaeton**  A form of dance music characterized by a fusion of Latin rhythms, dancehall and hip-hop.

**sampling**  The process of using sound clips from one musical piece in another musical piece.

**soul music**  A genre that originated in the African-American community that combines gospel music and jazz.

**sublime**  Inspiring great admiration or awe.

**sui generis**  Unique, belonging to a class of its own.

**syncopation**  A temporary displacement of the regular metrical accent in music caused by stressing the weak beat.

**trap music**  A genre of music popular in Southern hip-hop circles characterized by its bleak and gritty lyrical content.

**visibility**  The degree to which something is seen or understood by the public.

# Media Literacy Terms

"Media literacy" refers to the ability to access, understand, critically assess and create media. The following terms are important components of media literacy, and they will help you critically engage with the articles in this title.

**angle**  The aspect of a news story that a journalist focuses on and develops.

**attribution**  The method by which a source is identified or by which facts and information are assigned to the person who provided them.

**balance**  Principle of journalism that both perspectives of an argument should be presented in a fair way.

**byline**  Name of the writer, usually placed between the headline and the story.

**caption**  Identifying copy for a picture; also called a legend or cutline.

**column**  A type of story that is a regular feature, often on a recurring topic, written by the same journalist, generally known as a columnist.

**commentary**  A type of story that is an expression of opinion on recent events by a journalist generally known as a commentator.

**critical review**  A type of story that describes an event or work of art, such as a theater performance, film, concert, book, restaurant, radio or television program, exhibition or musical piece, and offers critical assessment of its quality and reception.

**editorial**  Article of opinion or interpretation.

**feature story**  Article designed to entertain as well as to inform.

**impartiality**  Principle of journalism that a story should not reflect a journalist's bias and should contain balance.

**intention**  The motive or reason behind something, such as the publication of a news story.

**interview story**  A type of story in which the facts are gathered primarily by interviewing another person or persons.

**motive**  The reason behind something, such as the publication of a news story or a source's perspective on an issue.

**news story**  An article or style of expository writing that reports news, generally in a straightforward fashion and without editorial comment.

**op-ed**  An opinion piece that reflects a prominent individual's opinion on a topic of interest.

**paraphrase**  The summary of an individual's words, with attribution, rather than a direct quotation of their exact words.

**quotation**  The use of an individual's exact words indicated by the use of quotation marks and proper attribution.

**reliability**  The quality of being dependable and accurate, said of a journalistic source.

**source**  The origin of the information reported in journalism.

**style**  A distinctive use of language in writing or speech; also a news or publishing organization's rules for consistent use of language with regards to spelling, punctuation, typography and capitalization, usually regimented by a house style guide.

**tone**  A manner of expression in writing or speech.

# Media Literacy Questions

**1.** Identify the various sources cited in the article "The New Face of Hip-Hop" (on page 135). How does Jon Caramanica attribute information to each of these sources in his article? How effective are Caramanica's attributions in helping the reader identify his sources?

**2.** In "The Passion of Nicki Minaj" (on page 66), Vanessa Grigoriadis directly quotes Nicki Minaj. What are the strengths of the use of a direct quote as opposed to a paraphrase? What are the weaknesses?

**3.** Compare the headlines of "Jay Z and Beyoncé: Activism Gone Vocal" (on page 39) and "In the Name of Cardi, Let Us Pray" (on page 171). Which is a more compelling headline, and why? How could the less compelling headline be changed to better draw the reader's interest?

**4.** What type of story is "Jay-Z and the Politics of Rapping in Middle Age" (on page 47)? Can you identify another article in this collection that is the same type of story?

**5.** Does Lizzy Goodman demonstrate the journalistic principle of impartiality in her article "Kendrick Lamar, Hip-Hop's Newest Old-School Star" (on page 91)? If so, how did she do so? If not, what could Goodman have included to make her article more impartial?

**6.** The article "The Heartbreak of Kanye West" (on page 204) is an example of an op-ed. Identify how Dream Hampton's attitude and tone help convey her opinion on the topic.

**7.** Does "Jay-Z Is Rhyming Picasso and Rothko" (on page 35) use multiple sources? What are the strengths of using multiple sources in a journalistic piece? What are the weaknesses of relying heavily on only one source or a few sources?

**8.** "Nicki Minaj's 'The Pinkprint' " (on page 53) is an example of a critical review. What is the purpose of a critical review? Do you feel this article achieved that purpose?

**9.** "Behind Kanye's Mask" (on page 182) is an example of an interview. What are the benefits of providing readers with direct quotes of an interviewed subject's speech? Is the subject of an interview always a reliable source?

**10.** What is the intention of the article "How Cardi B's 'Bodak Yellow' Took Over the Summer" (on page 160)? How effectively does it achieve its intended purpose?

**11.** Often, as a news story develops, a journalist's attitude toward a subject may change. Compare "Kanye West, Flaunting Pain Instead of Flash" (on page 178) and "Kanye West's Year of Breaking Bad" (on page 198), both by Jon Caramanica. Did new information discovered between the publication of these two articles change Caramanica's perspective?

# Citations

All citations in this list are formatted according to the Modern Language Association's (MLA) style guide.

## BOOK CITATION

THE NEW YORK TIMES EDITORIAL STAFF. *Influential Hip-Hop Artists.* New York: New York Times Educational Publishing, 2019.

## ONLINE ARTICLE CITATIONS

CARAMANICA, JON. "The Anxiety of Being Influential." *The New York Times,* 16 Sept. 2009, www.nytimes.com/2009/09/17/arts/music/17jayz.html.

CARAMANICA, JON. "Behind Kanye's Mask." *The New York Times,* 11 June 2013, www.nytimes.com/2013/06/16/arts/music/kanye-west-talks-about-his -career-and-album-yeezus.html.

CARAMANICA, JON. "Cardi B Is a New Rap Celebrity Loyal to Rap's Old Rules on 'Invasion of Privacy.' " *The New York Times,* 10 Apr. 2018, www.nytimes.com/2018/04/10/arts/music/cardi-b-invasion-of-privacy -review.html.

CARAMANICA, JON. "Drake: Rapper, Actor, Meme." *The New York Times,* 23 Oct. 2015, www.nytimes.com/2015/10/24/arts/music/drake-rapper-actor-meme .html.

CARAMANICA, JON. "How Cardi B's 'Bodak Yellow' Took Over the Summer." *The New York Times,* 23 Aug. 2017, www.nytimes.com/2017/08/23/arts /music/cardi-b-bodak-yellow.html.

CARAMANICA, JON. "Jay Z and Beyoncé: Activism Gone Vocal." *The New York Times,* 9 July 2016, www.nytimes.com/2016/07/09/arts/music/beyonce -jay-z-police-killings-spiritual.html.

CARAMANICA, JON. "Jay-Z Revels in the Catharsis of Confession on '4:44'." *The New York Times,* 2 July 2017, https://www.nytimes.com/2017/07/02 /arts/music/jay-z-4-44-review.html.

CARAMANICA, JON. "Kanye West, Flaunting Pain Instead of Flash." *The New York Times*, 24 Nov. 2008, www.nytimes.com/2008/11/25/arts/music /25kany.html.

CARAMANICA, JON. "Kanye West's Year of Breaking Bad." *The New York Times*, 5 Jan. 2017, www.nytimes.com/2017/01/05/arts/music/kanye-west -life-of-pablo-donald-trump.html.

CARAMANICA, JON. "Kendrick Lamar, Emboldened, but Burdened, by Success." *The New York Times*, 17 Mar. 2015, www.nytimes.com/2015/03/18/arts /music/kendrick-lamar-emboldened-but-burdened-by-success.html.

CARAMANICA, JON. "Kendrick Lamar, Rap's Skeptical Superstar, Avoids Arena Spectacle." *The New York Times*, 13 July 2017, https://www.nytimes.com /2017/07/13/arts/music/kendrick-lamar-damn-tour-review.html.

CARAMANICA, JON. "Kendrick Lamar's Anxiety Leads to Joy and Jabs on New Album." *The New York Times*, 16 Apr. 2017, www.nytimes.com/2017/04/16 /arts/music/kendrick-lamar-damn-review.html.

CARAMANICA, JON. "The New Face of Hip-Hop." *The New York Times*, 9 June 2010, www.nytimes.com/2010/06/13/arts/music/13drake.html.

CARAMANICA, JON. "Nicki Minaj and Meek Mill, Twitter's Ethics Police." *The New York Times*, 24 July 2015, www.nytimes.com/2015/07/25/arts/music /nicki-minaj-and-meek-mill-twitters-ethics-police.html.

CARAMANICA, JON. "Nicki Minaj Raps Life Lessons at Barclays Center." *The New York Times*, 27 July 2015, www.nytimes.com/2015/07/28/arts/music/review -nicki-minaj-raps-life-lessons-at-barclays-center.html.

CARAMANICA, JON. "Nicki Minaj's 'The Pinkprint.' " *The New York Times*, 15 Dec. 2014, www.nytimes.com/2014/12/16/arts/music/review -nicki-minajs-the-pinkprint.html.

CARAMANICA, JON. "On Drake's 'More Life,' the Creator Meets the Curator." *The New York Times*, 20 Mar. 2017, www.nytimes.com/2017/03/20/arts /music/drake-more-life-review.html.

CARAMANICA, JON. "On 'Views,' Drake Is Still His Own Genre." *The New York Times*, 29 Apr. 2016, www.nytimes.com/2016/04/30/arts/music/drake-views -album-review.html.

GAY, ROXANE. "Nicki Minaj, Always in Control." *The New York Times*, 16 Oct. 2017, www.nytimes.com/2017/10/16/t-magazine/nicki-minaj.html.

GOODMAN, LIZZY. "Kendrick Lamar, Hip-Hop's Newest Old-School Star." *The New York Times*, 25 June 2014, www.nytimes.com/2014/06/29/magazine /kendrick-lamar-hip-hops-newest-old-school-star.html.

GRIGORIADIS, VANESSA. "The Passion of Nicki Minaj." *The New York Times,* 7 Oct. 2015, www.nytimes.com/2015/10/11/magazine/the-passion-of-nicki -minaj.html.

HALBFINGER, DAVID M. "With Arena, Rapper Rewrites Celebrity Investors' Playbook." *The New York Times,* 15 Aug. 2012, www.nytimes.com/2012 /08/16/nyregion/with-the-nets-jay-z-rewrites-the-celebrity-investors -playbook.html.

HAMPTON, DREAM. "The Heartbreak of Kanye West." *The New York Times,* 7 May 2018, www.nytimes.com/2018/05/07/opinion/dream-hampton-kanye -west.html.

JAMES, MARLON. "The Blacker the Berry." *The New York Times,* 10 Mar. 2016, www.nytimes.com/interactive/2016/03/10/magazine/25-songs-that-tell-us -where-music-is-going.html#/kendrick-lamar-the-blacker-the-berry.

KAKUTANI, MICHIKO. "Jay-Z Deconstructs Himself." *The New York Times,* 22 Nov. 2010, www.nytimes.com/2010/11/23/books/23book.html.

KANG, JAY CASPIAN. "Notes on the Hip-Hop Messiah." *The New York Times,* 24 Mar. 2015, www.nytimes.com/2015/03/24/magazine/notes-on-the-hip -hop-messiah.html.

MORRIS, WESLEY. "Jay-Z and the Politics of Rapping in Middle Age." *The New York Times,* 19 July 2017, www.nytimes.com/2017/07/19/arts/music/jay-z -and-the-politics-of-rapping-in-middle-age.html.

NIKAS, JOANNA. "An Afternoon With Cardi B as She Makes Money Moves." *The New York Times,* 17 Aug. 2017, www.nytimes.com/2017/08/17/fashion /cardi-b-bodak-yellow.html.

PARELES, JON. "Kanye West Writes a Song of Himself on 'Ye.'" *The New York Times,* 3 June 2018, www.nytimes.com/2018/06/03/arts/music/kanye-west -ye-review.html.

PARELES, JON. "Kendrick Lamar Gives 'Black Panther' a Weighty Soundtrack." *The New York Times,* 14 Feb. 2018, https://www.nytimes.com/2018/02/14 /arts/music/kendrick-lamar-black-panther-soundtrack-review.html.

PARELES, JON, AND ZACHARY WOOLFE. "Kendrick Lamar Shakes Up the Pulitzer Game: Let's Discuss." *The New York Times,* 17 Apr. 2018, www.nytimes .com/2018/04/17/arts/music/kendrick-lamar-music-pulitzer-prize-damn.html.

ROGERS, KATIE. "Nicki Minaj: Black Women 'Rarely Rewarded' for Pop Cul- ture Contributions." *The New York Times,* 22 July 2015, www.nytimes.com /2015/07/23/arts/music/nicki-minaj-black-women-rarely-rewarded-for -pop-culture-contributions.html.

ROGERS, KATIE. "Nicki Minaj Concert in Angola Draws Human Rights Complaint." *The New York Times*, 16 Dec. 2015, www.nytimes.com/2015/12/17 /world/nicki-minaj-concert-in-angola-draws-human-rights-complaint.html.

SAFRONOVA, VALERIYA. "Cardi B Wins New York Fashion Week." *The New York Times*, 15 Feb. 2018, www.nytimes.com/2018/02/14/fashion/cardi-b -new-york-fashion-week.html.

SANNEH, KELEFA. "10 Years Wiser, Jay-Z Offers His Reflections of a Hustler." *The New York Times*, 27 June 2006, www.nytimes.com/2006/06/27/arts /music/27jayz.html.

SISARIO, BEN. "Cardi B Becomes the Fifth Female Rapper With a No. 1 Album." *The New York Times*, 16 Apr. 2018, www.nytimes.com/2018/04/16 /arts/music/cardi-b-invasion-of-privacy-billboard-chart.html.

SISARIO, BEN. "Drake's 'Scorpion' Is a Streaming Giant." *The New York Times*, 2 Jul. 2018, https://www.nytimes.com/2018/07/02/arts/music/drake -scorpion-streaming-records.html.

SMITH, ZADIE. "The House That Hova Built." *The New York Times*, 6 Sept. 2012, www.nytimes.com/2012/09/09/t-magazine/the-house-that-hova-built.html.

TREBAY, GUY. "Jay-Z Is Rhyming Picasso and Rothko." *The New York Times*, 12 July 2013, www.nytimes.com/2013/07/14/fashion/jay-z-is-rhyming -picasso-and-rothko.html.

WEAVER, CAITY. "In the Name of Cardi, Let Us Pray." *The New York Times*, 8 May 2018, www.nytimes.com/2018/05/08/style/cardi-b-met-gala.html.

WRIGHT, COLLEEN. "Kendrick Lamar, Rapper Who Inspired a Teacher, Visits a High School That Embraces His Work." *The New York Times*, 8 June 2015, www.nytimes.com/2015/06/09/nyregion/kendrick-lamar-rapper-who -inspired-a-teacher-visits-a-high-school-that-embraces-his-work.html.

# Index

*This book is current up until the time of printing. For the most up-to-date reporting, visit www.nytimes.com.*